Antique Trader®

CAMERAS
AND PHOTOGRAPHICA
PRICE GUIDE

Edited by

Kyle Husfloen

Contributing Editors
Bryan & Page Ginns

©2004 by Krause Publications

Published by

krause publications
An imprint of F+W Publications, Inc.

700 East State Street • Iola, WI 54990-0001
715-445-2214 • 888-457-2873
www.krause.com

Our toll-free number to place an order or obtain
a free catalog is (800) 258-0929.

Library of Congress Catalog Number: 0-87349-820-8
ISBN: 2004103291

Designed by Sandi Morrison and Wendy Wendt
Edited by Kyle Husfloen

Printed in U.S.A.

Table of Contents

Introduction

Nearly everyone today cherishes special photographs of family, friends or special events. In this fast-paced computerized 21st century it is difficult to imagine that there was a time when such images were unheard of. Some two centuries ago print illustrations and expensive oil paintings were available only to the well to do; there were few personal images available to the working classes until the 19th century.

Since old photographic images and equipment are still so abundant, it is our hope that this new *Antique Trader Cameras and Photographica Price Guide* will help to educate the collecting public. Many old snapshots and the cameras that took them have only sentimental value. This new reference, however, will provide an excellent overview of the most collectible photo-related equipment and images (collectively referred to as "photographica") on the market today.

Because we are covering nearly two hundred years of photographic history, our material is divided into specific chapters. In the first portion of this guide we will include listings and illustrations of photographic equipment of the past, including Cameras, Magic Lanterns & Optical Toys, and Stereoscopes & Viewers. Also included with these are listings of related accessories and images.

The latter portion of this guide includes listings and illustrations of the most collectible photographic images of the past. These listings are arranged alphabetically by the name of the category of image rather than in chronological order. Although we describe each of these image types in our Glossary of Selected Photographic Terms, I'll list them briefly here with their approximate dates of popularity:

Ambrotypes (ca. 1850s)
Autochromes (early 20th c.)
Cabinet Cards (ca. 1880s+)
Cartes-de-Visite (ca. 1860s)
Daguerreotypes (ca. 1840s-50s)
Tintypes (ca. 1860s-1900+)

With nearly 1,600 individual listings and more than 1,340 photographs, as well as a special 16-page full-color section, this new book will prove an invaluable reference for

"Heidoscope" Stereo Reflex Camera $2,250.

everyone in the collecting world, whether collector, dealer or appraiser.

We are also pleased to provide a special introductory feature on the history of photographica collecting by noted expert and dealer Bryan Ginns. Without his invaluable assistance this book would not have been possible. Bryan and his wife, Page, provide wonderful information on this topic at their Web site, www.stereographica.com. Be sure and check it out.

In this age of digital photography there may come a time when images produced with the aid of film negatives may fade away. Therefore this seems like an opportune time to collect and preserve all the photographic images of the past as well as the equipment used to produce and display them. They represent one of the major technological innovations of the past two centuries and will only grow more precious as the decades roll by.

I hope you enjoy the fruits of our efforts in producing the *Antique Trader Cameras and Photographica Price Guide* and that it will become an important part of your reference library. As always, I'll welcome your letters and comments and do my best to respond to them in a timely manner.

— Kyle Husfloen, Editor

Please note: Though listings have been double-checked and every effort has been made to ensure accuracy, neither the compilers, editors nor publisher can assume responsibility for any losses that might be incurred as a result of consulting this guide, or of errors, typographical or otherwise.

Collecting Antique Photographica

by Bryan Ginns

Antique Photographica is perhaps unique among all collectibles in that it encompasses both art and science. It was the Frenchman Louis Jacques Mandé Daguerre (1787-1851) who, through a combination of optics and chemistry, first perfected the process of obtaining a permanent image on silver plated copper and introduced it to the world in 1839.

Even today the image resulting from this process carries the inventor's name: "Daguerreotype." To be sure, many earlier experimenters and contributors worked in this area, but Daguerre is considered by many to be the father of photography.

The Daguerreotype was quickly followed by the Ambrotype and Tintype, both results of less expensive processes. Together with the Daguerreotype, these are collectively referred to today as "hard images." They have in common the fact that each image is one-of-a-kind, since no negatives are produced in these processes from which to print additional copies.

Their uniqueness presents a challenge to those attempting to put a value on these collectibles. The Daguerreotype is probably the most desirable of the hard images, reflected in prices ranging from about $20 to many thousands of dollars. The photographer, subject matter, aesthetic appeal and, of course, condition all affect values. Ambrotypes and Tintypes usually command significantly lower prices since images resulting from both these later processes are generally underrated by collectors. On the other hand, this assures that many interesting and highly collectible images remain available to collectors of modest means.

The invention of the *collodian* (wet plate) process in 1848 by the Englishman Frederick Scott Archer (1813-1857) was a major step forward. The Ambrotype and Tintype were produced using this process, but its greatest contribution was that it led to the development of glass plate negatives from which positive paper prints could be produced. This led to the manufacture of photographs for the masses: Cartes de Visite, Cabinet Cards, Stereoscopic Views and larger format photographs.

Opportunities to build a collection in these formats abound. Only in recent years have collectors realized the wealth of material available in the Carte de Visite and Cabinet Card formats. Value in these categories also depends on subject matter, photographer and condition.

Stereoscopic views, sold in the millions, might be among the most interesting images to collect, documenting as they do a history of America from about 1860 to the 1930s: the Civil War, western expansion, railroads, disasters, Expositions, the Spanish-American War and the Great War are all covered in great detail. It is difficult to come up with an important event or subject during this period that wasn't covered in stereoscopic

Right, from top: Ambrotype, sixth-plate Daguerreotype, Tintype, and quarter-plate Daguerreotype

Left, from top: Autochrome, Carte de Visite, Cabinet Card.
Above: Daguerreotype stereo view.

format. Individual views start at around a dollar or two, but rare views have been known to fetch a few thousand dollars.

In about 1900 several publishers introduced boxed sets of 50 or 100 views covering various subjects or geographical locations. These represent good value for collectors since complete sets of 100 typically sell for $300 to $800 depending on the locations or subjects represented. Some rarer sets sell for considerably more.

Another area of growing collector interest is the Autochrome, the image resulting from the first commercially viable color process patented by the Lumiére Brothers in 1904. Fine examples of this early color process are not easy to find.

While 19th and 20th century "art" photographs in larger formats are eagerly collected, they are outside the scope of this price guide.

Cameras and other equipment from the Daguerreian and collodian eras are keenly sought after and generally tend to command high prices for good examples. Cameras from the last half of the 19th century are highly collectible. During this period the technology advanced from plates to roll film. Beautifully made wood and brass cameras, box types, stereoscopic, detective and spy cameras continued to be developed and offered by enterprising individuals and companies. By the end of the 19th century George Eastman was successfully marketing his "Kodak" brand of cameras to the masses.

From left: English sliding box camera, ca. 1855-60; British Ferrotype Co. Telephot Tintype Button camera, ca. 1910; Stirn concealed vest camera, ca. 1886.

ICA (Zeiss) Ideal stereo camera, ca. 1930.

This period also witnessed an explosion of technical advances resulting in smaller hand-held cameras for roll film, color photography and the birth of cinematic photography. The invention of the 35mm film format eventually led to the development of miniature cameras by the great European manufacturers such as Leica, Zeiss and many others through the pre-World War II period.

In the immediate postwar period German optics retained their dominant position in the marketplace. Japanese 35mm cameras during this period had a rather poor reputation. From the mid-1950s, however, Japanese camera makers have dominated the market in the United States through constant innovation, lower production costs and improved optics. This dominance has continued into today's digital photography era.

With patience it is still possible to build a good general collection of antique photographic hardware. In recent years, however, more specialized collections have evolved. Camera collectors might concentrate on specific time periods, for example cameras and lenses made in the 19th century. They might specialize in a particular type of camera: stereoscopic, detective and spy, subminiature, 35mm cameras and so forth. Still other collectors will focus on a particular maker such as Leica or Kodak. Even something as specialized as postwar Japanese range-finder cameras are enthusiastically collected.

Stereoscopes represent another collecting opportunity. It is only in recent years that individuals have developed an interest in these views. The early stereoscope designs of Sir Charles Wheatstone (1802-1875) and Sir David Brewster (1781-1868) eventually led to an explosion in the demand for stereoscopes and stereoscopic views. This was particularly true in England when Queen Victoria expressed great interest after seeing them on display at the Great Exhibition of 1851. During this period the parlor stereoscope became the main source of entertainment in every well-to-do home.

Viewing historic three-dimensional images in a stereoscope still amazes people even in this era of personal computers, video games and digitized images. There are scores of different patent designs, mainly from the United States, England and France. It is still possible to build a representative collection ranging from rare early viewers of the 1850s to View Masters of the 1950s.

Other antique photographic collectibles that are gaining in popularity are magic lanterns, lantern slides, optical toys and other pre-cinema items. These include rare early "persistence of vision" items such as the Thaumotrope, Phenakistoscope, Zoetrope, and the Praxinoscope.

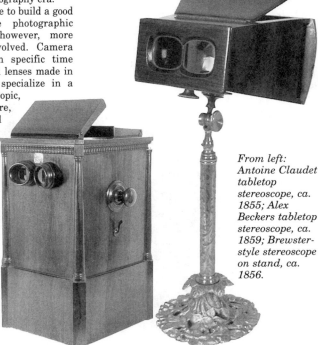

From left: Antoine Claudet tabletop stereoscope, ca. 1855; Alex Beckers tabletop stereoscope, ca. 1859; Brewster-style stereoscope on stand, ca. 1856.

"Jung Amerika" Magic Lantern, ca. 1880s.

McLoughlin Bros. "Whirligig of Life" Praxinoscope, ca. 1880s.

These and other similar inventions are among the earliest experiments designed for animation. It would be the end of the 19th century before a true motion picture camera and projector would be widely available.

Micro-photographs mounted in Stanhopes (special novelty-shaped viewers) are also considered photographic collectibles. Surprisingly perhaps, the Kaleidoscope also has an antique photographic connection: the inventor of both the Kaleidoscope and the refracting stereoscope was Scottish physicist Sir David Brewster.

The most important asset for any collector is not wealth but patience. Very few if any of these antique photographic items are truly unique, except, of course, for the "hard images" mentioned earlier. A good collection cannot be built overnight, but given time an interesting and enjoyable collection can be assembled. You probably should not acquire these items if investment and the expectation of ever increasing value is the first priority; you can never be certain that *any* collectible will increase in value. Buy the item because you enjoy it; if it does increase in value, consider it a bonus.

One final caveat: always try to buy the best quality you can afford. An apparent bargain of questionable condition or quality rarely turns out to be a sound acquisition over the long term.

Bryan Ginns is a noted authority and dealer in photographica. He can be reached at 2109 Route 21, Valatie, NY 12184, phone (518) 392-5805, fax (518) 392-7925, or visit the Web at www.stereographica. com.

Pipe-shaped Stanhope, early 20th century.

Zoetrope, ca. 1872.

"Le Phenakisticope," ca. 1850.

Brewster Patent Kaleidoscope telescoping model, ca. 1818, with cells.

CHAPTER 1
Cameras

Al Vista Panoramic Camera

Al Vista Panoramic camera, by Multiscope & Film Co. of Burlington, Wisconsin, Model 5B, comes w/all five fans to control speed & original view finder, rare, ca. 1905 (ILLUS.)... **$250**

American Optical/Scovill Camera

American Optical/Scovill Camera

American Optical/Scovill Mfg. Co. view camera w/Flammang's 1883 patent revolving back, w/brass-barreled J.H. Dallmeyer 8 1/2 x 6 1/2" Rapid Rectilinear lens, three original double dark slides, red bellows, lens panel marked "American Optical Co., Scovill Mfg. Co." (ILLUS., right column, top) **350**

Anthony "Gem" Tintype Camera

Anthony (E. & H.) "Gem" tintype camera, nine-lens version, the ground focusing screen measures 6" x 6", internal septum for nine "Gem" tintype images, original bellows, overall excellent condition, ca. 1870 (ILLUS.)... **3,410**

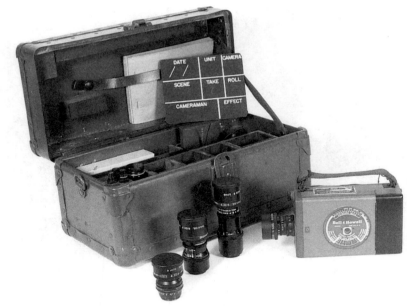

Camera Outfit Made for U.S. Army

Anthony Ferrotype Camera

Anthony View Camera & Accessories

Anthony Ferrotype camera, wooden case, four-tube model, America, ca. 1870s (ILLUS.) **2,000-3,000**

Anthony view camera, 5 x 8" view-type, quality brass-bound Darlot lens w/slot for Waterhouse stops, w/an early fully functional mechanical shutter patent-dated 1888, a Scovill & Adams No. 2 Magic Finder in original box & a set of Waterhouse stops, all in the original wooden box, the group (ILLUS. next column) **450**

Bell & Howell Cine outfit, aluminum, khaki & black colored as it was made for U.S. Army during World War II, uses 16 mm magazines, outfit consists of camera, four (.7", 1", 2" & 4") lenses w/matching viewfinders, complete set of filters, chalk board, original chalk, lens-cleaning tissue, all in fitted combat-style case, metal plate on outside reads "Camera Set, Motion Picture KS-11(1) Mfg. No. 08481, Order no. AF-33 (600)25103, Bell & Howell Company, U.S. Property," rare, mint (ILLUS. top of page) **365**

Rare "Camera Lite" Cigarette Lighter Spy Camera

Blair "Kameret" of 1891

Blair "Kameret," leather box case w/internal stops & fully operational

shutter, w/a plate back, focusing screen & a double dark slide (plate holder), the roll film back not included, leather a little dry w/signs of wear, ca. 1891, 4 x 5" (ILLUS.).. 650

Bloch "Physiographe" monocular detective camera, half-round black crinkled finish, designed to resemble a monocular, takes the picture at right angle to the viewfinder, minimal signs of wear, shutter sticks slightly, ca. 1910 .... **1,000**

British Airways novelty camera, printed metal in the shape of a bulbous jet airliner, mint condition in original box........... **110**

"Camera Lite" spy camera, Model B, camera disguised in a Zippo lighter, w/instructions, case & original box, near mint (ILLUS. top of page)............................ **700**

Carmen "Pygmee" Camera

"Coronet 3-D Camera" & Original Box

Rare 1870s Camera Obscura

Camera obscura, brass w/original lacquer & flange, multi-angle lens, rare, France, ca. 1870s (ILLUS.) **950**

German Camera Obscura

Camera obscura, covered in green cloth w/worn gilt embossing reading "Camera Obscura Zeichen - Apparat," Germany, late 19th c., stains, tape reinforcements, camera 8 x 10", 6" h. (ILLUS.) **200**

Carmen "Pygmee" camera, Bakelite-type case, mint condition in original box, Germany, ca. 1930 (ILLUS. bottom of previous page) **885**

Chapman stereoscopic camera, mahogany & brass half-plate model, original maroon bellows, correct lens w/septum present, by J.T. Chapman, Manchester, England, late 19th c. **1,450**

Comet III Camera from Italy

Comet III camera, by Bencini of Milan, uses 127 film, w/case, unusual, Italy, ca. 1953 (ILLUS.).. **40**

"Coronet 3-D Camera," takes stereoscopic pairs on 127 roll film, case in multicolored Bakelite, nearly mint in original box (ILLUS. top of page).. **65**

Coronet "Midget" camera, bright green Bakelite case, ca. 1935, excellent condition.. **250**

"Criterion" view camera outfit, by Gundlach Manhattan Optical Co., folding-type camera w/8 x 10" rapid Convertible lens, includes five double dark slides & eight film sheaths, all in the original fitted canvas case, also w/a Fomer & Schwing wooden tripod, ca. 1915, 8 x 10" (lens w/some balsaming) **275**

Optical Company, New York, New York, black leatherette case w/maroon bellows & fully working shutter, rear glass focusing screen cracked but replaceable, w/two double-sided plate holders in the original case, ca. 1905 (ILLUS.).................... **90**

1840s Daguerreotype Camera

Daguerreotype camera, w/chamfered wooden box, ca. 1840s (ILLUS.). **12,000-15,000**

Red Coronet "Midget" Camera

Coronet "Midget" camera, red Bakelite case, used 16mm film, excellent condition, ca. 1930s (ILLUS.)........................ **225**

"Cycle Wizard" Model A Camera

"Cycle Wizard" Model A camera, folding-type, for 5 x 4" plates, by the Manhattan

Duplex Super 120 Stereo Camera

Duplex Super 120 stereo camera, fully functional using 120 roll film, near mint condition w/original leather case, Italy, ca. 1955 (ILLUS.) **450**

E.R.A.C.
Mercury Pistol Subminiature Camera

E.R.A.C. Mercury pistol camera, black Bakelite housing, "Merlin" subminiature camera w/trigger mechanism to fire shutter & advance film, ca. 1938 (ILLUS.) **500**

"Eiko" Novelty Tire Camera

"Eiko" novelty tire camera, round tire-shaped plastic, for 110 film, made in Taiwan, ca. 1980s, new in original box (ILLUS.)... **30**

"Eho" German Stereo Box Camera

"Eho" stereo box camera, low rectangular case, fully operating shutter, uses 120 roll film, very fine condition, Germany, ca. 1933 (ILLUS.)... **275**

Ensign "Ful-Vue" Camera

Ensign "Ful-Vue" camera, available in black, grey, red or blue, England, ca. 1950s (ILLUS.).. **50-100**

Ensign "Midget"
Model 120
Camera & Box

Ensign "Midget"
Model 33
Camera & Box

Ensign "Midget" Model 22 camera, folding-type, black crinkled metal case, England, ca. 1930s, near mint condition in original box (ILLUS. bottom of previous page).. **88**

Ensign "Midget" Model 33 camera, folding-type, black crinkled metal case, England, ca. 1930s, near mint condition, w/case & instructions in original box (ILLUS. top of page)....................................... **94**

Ernemann "Stereo Ernoflex" Camera

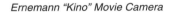

Ernemann "Kino" Movie Camera

Ernemann "Kino" hand-crank movie camera, oak, 35 mm, operational shutter/film transport mechanism, incorrect lens, front element of viewfinder missing (ILLUS. right column, top)............ **1,106**

Ernemann "Stereo Ernoflex" camera, for 45 x 107mm plates, w/f3 1/2 "Ernon" lenses, working focal plane shutter, comes w/magazine & camera case, rare, Germany, ca. 1925 (ILLUS. right, top) **1,300**

"Expo Police Camera," flat rectangular form w/cloth focal plane shutter & fixed focus lens w/two aperture settings, w/instructions in original box, excellent condition, ca. 1915 (ILLUS. right column, bottom)... **900**

"Expo Police Camera"

Field camera, walnut & brass, w/metal plaque indicating camera is from establishment of "C. Merville, Paris," ca. 1890s **330**

Gaumont Stereo-Block-Notes Camera

Gaumont Stereo-Block-Notes camera, for 45 x 107mm plates, w/one plate holder, fully operating shutter, excellent condition, France, ca. 1920 (ILLUS.) **375**

Griffiths "Guinea" detective camera, quarter plate model, upright rectangular black case, flip-up top, w/twelve metal plate holders, England, ca. 1895, very fine condition **375**

Happy Clown Novelty Camera

"Happy Clown Camera," novelty plastic clown face, for 110 film, new in original plastic bubble display pack (ILLUS.) **20**

"Heidoscope" Stereo Reflex Camera

"Heidoscope" stereo reflex camera, by Franke & Heidecke, matched Zeiss F4.5 Tessar lenses, w/the magazine plate holder & rare 120 roll film back, fully operational w/original fitted leather case, Germany, ca. 1930 (ILLUS.) **2,250**

Houghton's "Ticka" novelty watch camera, w/instructions in original box, ca. 1905 (ILLUS. bottom of page) **500**

Hüttig Box Camera

Houghton's "Ticka" Watch Camera

Hüttig "GNOM" falling plate magazine box camera, metal, w/six 4 1/2 x 6mm internal plate holders, rare small version, crack in top of viewfinder glass, 2 x 3 x 4" (ILLUS.) **302**

ICA (Zeiss) Stereo Ideal Camera

ICA (Zeiss) Stereo Ideal camera, folding-type in black leatherette case, Model 650 for 9 x 18cm plates, working compound shutter, w/a pair of "Hekla" f6.8 lenses, signs of use but overall very good condition, ca. 1930 (ILLUS.) **250**

"1892 Instantograph Patent" Field Camera

"Instantograph 1892 Patent" field camera, 1/2 plate type, w/original lacquered brass & bright red bellows, comes w/one double dark slide, J. Lancaster, England (ILLUS.) **360**

French Stereoscopic Camera

Jonte (F.) stereoscopic camera, walnut case, maroon tapering bellows, fully working shutter assembly, slots for internal septum, w/original canvas carrying bag, France, missing internal septum, ca. 1900 (ILLUS.) **1,100**

Kershaw Stereoscopic Reflex Camera

Kershaw Stereoscopic Reflex camera, 3 x 5" model w/Taylor Hobson f4.5 lenses, shutter speeds to 1/700th of a second, includes the retailer's label for J.C. McKechnie - Optician, 31a Castle St. Edinburgh, w/two double dark slides in leather case, excellent condition, ca. 1910 (ILLUS.) **1,600**

Miniature Cameras

Keystone F-8 Aircraft Camera

Keystone F-8 Aircraft Camera, made by the Keystone Mfg. Co., Boston, Massachusetts, w/an f5.6 Wollensak 15" telephoto lens, takes a 5" x 7" image on special roll film 7" wide x 25' long, focal plane shutter w/speeds ranging from 1/125th to 1/500th of a second, comes w/a restricted document 72 page instruction & parts catalog dated January 1, 1944, was to be used to render service to the United States or its Allies, w/a No. 12 minus blue filter in original military-style box, used for nationally sensitive aerial reconnaissance & probably not commercial use, ca. 1940s, near mint (ILLUS.)... **220**

Kiev-Vega subminiature "spy" camera, disguised as a pack of John Player Special cigarettes, some doubt as to whether this was made for the KGB or for the collector market, Russia (ILLUS. top of page, center w/miniature cameras) **500**

"King's Own" Tropical Camera

1950s Kodak 35mm Stereo Camera

Kin-Dar Stereo Camera

Kin-Dar stereo camera, 35mm type, F3.5 Steinhell Cassar lenses, fully functional shutter w/speeds from 1/10 to 1/200 of a second, includes leather case, ca. 1954 (ILLUS.).. **80**

"King's Own" tropical camera outfit, by London Stereoscopic Company, teak w/brass inlay & a 180mm f6.8 Goertz Dagor lens w/a B & L "Volute" shutter, includes both the roll film & plate backs & separate focusing screen, & two double dark slides, all enclosed in two fitted leather cases w/company label, overall excellent condition, ca. 1905, the set (ILLUS. bottom of previous page) **2,100**

Kodak 35mm stereo camera, nearly mint in original box w/instructions, ca. 1955 (ILLUS. top of page)..................................... **170**

Kodak "50th Anniversary" camera, mint in original box w/minor tears **200**

Kodak Beau Brownie No. 2 camera, brown, ca. 1930 (ILLUS. bottom of page, right w/other Beau Brownies)......................... **85**

Kodak Beau Brownie No. 2A camera, black, ca. 1930 (ILLUS. bottom of page, left w/other Beau Brownies) **93**

Kodak Beau Brownie No. 2A camera, rose pink, made by "Canadian Kodak Co. Limited," rare in this color & by this maker, ca. 1930, shutter not working (ILLUS. bottom of page, center w/other Beau Brownies)... **365**

Kodak Beau No. 2 Brownie camera, box-type, blue w/original handle at the top, excellent condition, ca. 1930 (minor split in one end of handle) **120**

Kodak Beau Brownie Cameras

Kodak Boy Scout Camera

Kodak Boy Scout camera, folding-type, English model, w/the original black bellows & both the face & shutter plates differing from the American model, excellent condition w/original green leather cased w/embossed Scout logo, ca. 1930 (ILLUS.) **350**

English Boy Scout & Girl Guide Cameras

Kodak Boy Scout camera, original black bellows matches black lens/shutter plate, in matching case, England, ca. 1930 (ILLUS. left w/Girl Guide camera) **305**
Kodak Boy Scout U.S.A. Model folding camera, black leatherette case, large Boy Scout logo on enameled back, fully working shutter & original green bellows, w/original instructions & matching leather case w/logo, overall excellent condition, ca. 1930 (ILLUS. bottom of page) **215**

1950s Kodak Brownie Flash B Camera

Kodak Brownie Flash B box camera, near mint condition w/original case, ca. 1950s (ILLUS.) **35**

Kodak Brownie Flash IV camera, box-type, two-tone brown & tan case, nearly mint condition in original canvas case (ILLUS. top of next page) **26**

Kodak Bullet "New York World's Fair" camera, sold only in 1939-40, overall excellent condition **350**

Kodak Boy Scout Camera
with Case & Instructions

Kodak Brownie Flash IV Camera

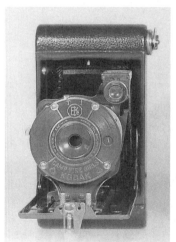

box but missing the lipstick & compact, camera in excellent condition, the set (ILLUS. top of next page) **500**

English Kodak Girl Guide Camera

Kodak Girl Guide camera, folding-type, Girl Guide logo on side, original black bellows, matching blue case, couple of very minor chips on face plate, overall very good condition, England, ca. 1930 (ILLUS.) **300**

Kodak Girl Guide camera, original blue bellows in matching case, scarce, England, ca. 1930 (ILLUS. right w/Boy Scout camera) **300**

Front & Back of Kodak Camp Fire Girls Camera

Kodak Camp Fire Girls camera, folding-type w/leatherette case & metal printed w/the Camp Fire Girls logo, black bellows, matching case, excellent condition, rare (ILLUS. front and back) **2,250**

Kodak "Ensemble" camera outfit, folding-type, beige clamshell-style case, original beige bellows, w/instructions in original

Kodak "Ensemble"
Camera Outfit

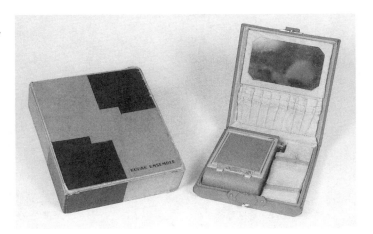

Scout logo, original green bellows,
w/matching case, slight signs of wear,
minor scratch on face plate (ILLUS.) **325**
**Kodak Hawk-Eye No. 2 Film Pack
advertising camera,** box-type, black
leatherette case printed on the end "Drink
First Aid," w/original box & an original
advertising poster, the group (ILLUS. top
of next page) **350**

Kodak Hawkette No. 2 Camera
Kodak Hawkette No. 2 camera, mottled
brown Bakelite, scarce in this excellent
condition, England, ca. 1930s (ILLUS.) **99**

Two Views of Kodak Girl Scout Camera
Kodak Girl Scout camera, folding-type,
black leather & metal printed w/the Girl

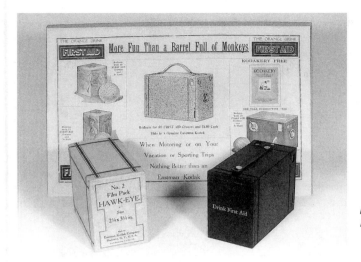

*Kodak Hawk-Eye
No. 2 Advertising
Box Camera*

mounts, rolls of exposed (?) film &
instructions in Italian, for the Italian
market, overall excellent condition, ca.
1900, the group (ILLUS.) **550**

Silver Jubilee Camera

Kodak No. 2 Brownie, silver, sold during
1935 Silver Jubilee celebrations for King
George V & Queen Mary, rare (ILLUS.)....... **225**

Kodak No. 2 Brownie camera, box-type,
by Kodak Ltd., England, brown case
w/black metal trim, overall excellent
condition, ca. 1930s (some rust spots on
film door clip)... **40**

Kodak No. 2 Brownie camera, box-type,
grey case w/black metal trim, w/portrait
attachment, England, ca. 1930s, camera
very good condition, box a little weak
w/interior taping (ILLUS. top of next
page)... **151**

Kodak No. 1 Brownie Camera Outfit

Kodak No. 1 Brownie camera outfit,
Model B, includes the camera w/canvas
case, Brownie developing tank in original
distressed box, three developing trays, a
Kodak printing frame, a Kodak
measuring beaker, chemicals, six photo

Kodak Brownie No. 2 Camera with Box

*No. 2 Brownie
Royal Commemorative Camera*

Kodak No. 2 Brownie camera, box-type, silver-colored case, manufactured & issued only in Great Britain in 1935 for the Silver Jubilee of King George V & Queen Mary, some surface soiling, overall excellent condition (ILLUS.)............. **190**

Kodak No. 2 Folding Brownie Camera

Kodak No. 2 Brownie Model A camera, folding-type, black leatherette case, maroon bellows, fully working shutter, near mint condition, ca. 1904 (ILLUS.) **85**

Kodak No. 2 Stereo Brownie Camera

Kodak No. 2 Stereo Brownie, folding-type, black leather exterior, red bellows, ca. 1905 (ILLUS.).. **400**

Kodak No. 2A Cartridge Hawk-Eye Model B camera, box-type, mint condition w/original box w/slight wear (ILLUS. top of next page) **130**

Kodak No. 2A Rainbow - Hawk-Eye camera, green case, in a marked Special Hawk-Eye Combination Package box, includes the camera, three rolls of 116 roll film & a Kodakery subscription & instructions, box w/corner wear, camera excellent... **150**

*Kodak No. 2A
Cartridge Hawk-Eye
Model B with
Original Box*

Kodak "Tim's Official Camera"

Kodak No. 2A Rainbow Hawkeye "Tim's Official Camera," box-type, red leatherette case, ca. 1930s, scarce, very good condition (ILLUS.) **260**

Fine Kodak "Tim's Official Camera"

Kodak No. 2A Rainbow Hawkeye "Tim's Official Camera," box-type, w/decal on side, ca. 1930s, rare in this condition w/logo virtually 100 percent intact (ILLUS.).. **330**

No. 3A Panoram Kodak Camera

Kodak No. 3A Panoram camera, one of the least common of the Panoram series, ca. 1927, shutter a little sticky on slow speed (ILLUS.)...................................... **350**

Kodak No. 3A Panoram Camera

Kodak No. 3A Panoram camera, self-contained in rectangular black leatherette case, full working order, w/a reproduction of the original instructions, ca. 1926 (ILLUS.).................... **325**

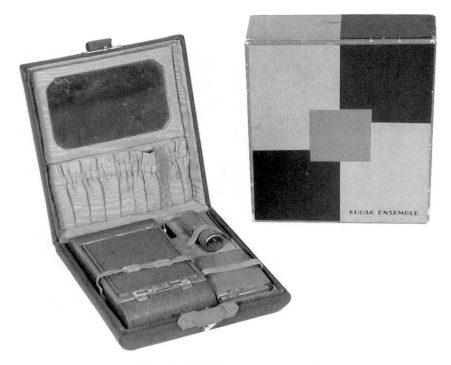

Rare Kodak Petite Camera Ensemble

Kodak No. 4 Screen Focus Model A

Kodak No. 4 Screen Focus Model A camera, w/fully working Kodak Automatic shutter w/speeds from 1 to 1/100 of a second, plus B. & T. Bausch & Lomb f4.0 Rapid Rectilinear lens, the cherry wood interior w/red bellows, w/original matching carrying case, ca. 1900 (ILLUS.)... **475**

Kodak Petite Camera Ensemble outfit, includes folding camera w/working shutter but somewhat dry bellows, a compact & tube of lipstick, all in green suede case w/a mirror inside the top, push-pull pins used to extend the bed of the camera very weak, some wear to case exterior & some lipstick stains inside, overall very good condition, rare set, ca. 1930 (ILLUS. top of page) **1,200**

Kodak Pocket '96 Model Camera

Kodak Pocket '96 Model, box-type, w/instructions & original box, appears to be one of the later models (ILLUS.) **225**

Kodak Portrait Brownie No. 2 Camera with Box

Kodak Portrait Brownie No. 2 camera, box-type, maroon, in original box, box worn w/tape re-enforcement (ILLUS. top of page) **440**

Kodak Six-20 B camera, w/Compur shutter & f4 1/2 Anastigmat lens, leather case, instructions, original box (ILLUS. bottom of page) **45**

Kodak stereo camera, 35mm, comes w/instruction booklet in original box, ca. 1955 (ILLUS. top of next page) **180**

Kodak Stereo Camera Model 1, folding-type w/fully operational Kodak Ball Bearing shutter, excellent condition, ca. 1916 (ILLUS. following) **325**

Kodak Stereo Camera Model 1

Kodak Six-20 B Camera with Box

Kodak 35mm Stereo Camera

"Lancaster, Stereo Instantograph" Camera

"Lancaster, Stereo Instantograph" camera, mahogany & brass, for 6 3/4 x 3 1/4" plates, matching Lancaster patent, brass-barreled lenses w/original lacquer, original black leather bellows, non-removable internal septum, comes w/three double dark slides & original black focusing cloth, J. Lancaster, England, ca. 1891 (ILLUS.)...................... **1,800**

Detective Camera Disguised as Handbag

Lancaster "Folding Instantograph" detective camera, quarter-plate type, disguised as woman's handbag, covered in black leather w/embossed gilt highlights, w/two double dark slides, rare, J. Lancaster, England, ca. 1893 (ILLUS.) . **2,750**

"Le Franceville" Camera

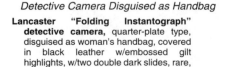

Linex Stereo Camera &
Viewer Outfit

"Le Franceville" camera, papier-mâché, for 4 x 4cms glass plates, w/viewfinder, original excellent condition, France, ca. 1910 (ILLUS. on previous page, from back) **300**

Liesegang Field Camera

Liesegang field camera, wood & brass, 17 x 12cm format, green canvas bellows w/original maroon leather corner reinforcement, worm screw mechanism at rear extends bellows, brass-barreled "Rapid Aplanat, no. 1 Lens" by E. Suter, Basel, serial no. 7627, Germany, ca. 1900 (ILLUS.)... **375**

Linex Stereo Camera & Viewer outfit, all in original cardboard box w/case & instructions, also w/a couple of film magazines & numerous empty slide mounts, excellent condition, ca. 1950s, the set (ILLUS. top of page) **225**

Linex subminiature stereo camera outfit, w/camera, case, viewer & instruction booklet, in original box, ca. 1954 (ILLUS. bottom of page).. **250**

Lizars "Challenge" stereoscopic camera, Model B, folding-type, rectangular black leather-covered case w/nice red bellows, Bausch & Lomb stereo shutter sticks slightly, w/three double dark slides, all in original fitted leather case, J. Lizars, Scotland, ca. 1905 .... **750**

Linex Subminiature Stereo
Camera Outfit

Lizars "Challenge" Stereo Camera

Lizars "Challenge" stereoscopic camera,
Model B, w/Bausch & Lomb Rapid
Rectilinear lenses, original maroon
bellows, comes w/six double dark slides,
original dark cloth in fitted Lizars case
plus wooden tripod, J. Lizars,
Scotland, ca. 1905 (ILLUS.) **850**
Lizars "Tropical Challenge" camera,
folding-type, unusual smaller model in
Spanish mahogany case w/original red
bellows, fully working Bausch & Lomb
shutter & Rapid rectilinear lens, excellent
condition, J. Lizars, Scotland, ca. 1910,
2 1/2 x 3 1/2" **700**

English Binocular Camera &
Enlarging Camera

London   Stereoscopic   Company
binocular   camera   outfit,   Jules
Carpentier 1892 patent Photo Jumelle
under L.S.C. name, one lens for viewing,
one for taking single exposures on
4 1/2 x 6cm plates, ebony back, fully
working shutter, 12 of the original
numbered   plate   holders;   London
Stereoscopic   Co.   Patent   Daylight
Enlarging Camera, possibly walnut &
brass, w/three paddle-style filters, "Red
for use in foggy weather," "Yellow for use
in haze or mist," "Neutral for use in bright

sunlight," original fitted leather case,
London, England, ca. 1890s (ILLUS. of
binocular camera & enlarging camera) **500**

London Stereoscopic Company
Field Camera

London   Stereoscopic   Company   field
camera, tailboard-style stereo camera,
w/original black canvas bellows, pair of
consecutively numbered 7779 & 7780
Wray 4 1/4 x 3 1/4 lenses, 4" focal
length,   England, ca.   1895,   missing
septum (ILLUS.) **1,150**

Lumiere "Sterelux" No. 1 Camera

Lumiere   "Sterelux"   Model   1   camera,
folding-type in black leatherette case, roll
film stereo model w/Lumiere f4.5
"Spector"   working   lenses   w/speeds
from 1/25 to 1/100 of a second, includes
worn leather carrying case, camera in
excellent condition, France, ca. 1920s
(ILLUS.).. **225**
Magic "Photoret" novelty watch camera,
w/film can in original box, rare, ca. 1894
(ILLUS. top of next page)......................... **1,331**

Magic "Photoret" Watch Camera

Mandel "PDQ" Street Camera

Mandel "PDQ" Street Camera, for 2 x 3" prints, black leatherette & metal case, prints made from a continuous roll of direct positive film, includes Wollensak 114mm f4.5 Raptar lens & Betax No. 2 shutter w/speeds to 1/100th of a second, w/original developing tank & apparently original timer mounted on the side, works fine (ILLUS.) **300**

"Mandel-ette Post Card Camera"

"Mandel-ette Post Card Camera," by The Chicago Ferrotype Co., tintype street camera, 2 1/2 x 3 1/5" format, patented April 14, 1914 (ILLUS.) **140**

"Mighty - Gift Box" subminiature camera, w/a 2X telephoto attachment, lens hood, case, instructions & a box of roll film, all in original box, near mint, the set **300**

Mikroma I Stereo Camera

Mikroma I Stereo camera, using 16mm film in special cassettes, F3.5 "Mirar" lenses, fully working shutter w/speeds from 1/5 to 1/100 of a second, includes original leather case, lens caps & two empty cassettes, Czechoslovakia (ILLUS.) **180**

Stereo Mikroma Camera Outfit

Mikroma II Stereo Camera

Mikroma II stereo camera, fully functioning, also w/two cassettes for loading the 16mm film, slides can be mounted & viewed in the View Master format, w/original ever-ready case, made in Czechoslovakia, ca. 1965 (ILLUS.) **200**

Mikroma II stereo camera outfit, long, narrow camera w/a small tripod ring on the bottom plate, w/a cutter in excellent condition & a leather ever-ready case, used 16mm movie film in special cassettes, two cassettes included so

makes this subminiature camera fully useable in the View Master format, overall excellent condition, made in Czechoslovakia, ca. 1960, the set (ILLUS. top of page) **350**

Minolta 16MG camera outfit, includes silvered metal 35mm camera, case, flash, instructions, all in original presentation case, excellent condition, Japan (ILLUS. bottom of page) **43**

French Monobloc Stereo Camera

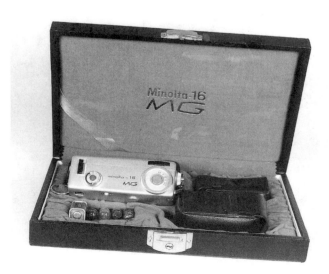

*Minolta 16MG
Camera Outfit*

Monobloc Stereo Camera, by Jeaneret & Cie., Paris, deluxe version w/tan leather & brushed nickel exterior, fully functional multi-speed shutter w/f3.5 Tessar lenses, original spirit level on top is dried out, w/two multi-plate magazines, all in the original worn leather case, France, ca. 1920s (ILLUS. previous page) **250**

Monroe Pocket #2 Camera

Monroe Pocket #2 camera, original red bellows in very good shape, America, ca. 1897 (ILLUS.).. **355**

"National Graflex" Series II Camera

"National Graflex" Series II camera, focal plane working shutter w/speeds to 1/500th of a second, B&L f3.5 Tessar lens, uses 120 roll film, excellent condition w/original black leather case, Graflex, Inc., United States (ILLUS.)............ **225**

Newman & Guardia "Nydia" Camera

Newman & Guardia "Nydia" camera, unusual folding-type, shutter speeds to 1/100th of a second w/an f6.3 Ross lens, original leather case, excellent condition, England, ca. 1900 (ILLUS.)....................... **1,350**

No. 1 Demon Detective Camera

No. 1 Demon Detective camera, embossed "The Demon Camera - The Wonder of the World - O'Reillys - Sole Manufacturers - The American Camera Co. - 399 Edgeware Road - London," England, ca. 1889 (ILLUS.)............. **1,500-2,500**

Owla Stereo Camera

French Panoramic-Stereo Camera

Owla stereo camera, 35mm type, F3.5 Owla lenses, fully working shutter w/speeds from 1/10 to 1/200 of a second, scarce, includes leather case, Japan, ca. 1958 (ILLUS. previous page) **275**

Panoramic-stereoscopic combination camera, panoramic lens is a Panorthoscopic No. 0 by Clement & Gilmer, stereo lens unmarked, string set roller blind shutter working, ground glass focusing screen & a folding eye-level viewfinder, original maroon bellows, overall excellent condition, France, ca. 1900 (ILLUS. top of page)........................ **1,864**

maroon bellows & P, S & R, Optimus 5 x 7" lens, w/double dark slide, England, ca. 1890 (ILLUS.)........................ **600**

"Petal" subminiature camera, scarce round shape, in original box w/instructions & film pack, ca. 1948 (ILLUS. right w/miniature cameras) **320**

"Photo Hall" French Stereo Camera

"Photo Hall" stereo camera, for 6 x 13cm plates, fully working shutter & interior sliding box-style focusing method, France, ca. 1910 (ILLUS.)............................ **500**

"Photo-See" camera outfit, box-type camera, includes camera, developing tank, film & developer, all in the original boxes, also five bottles for various chemicals & original instructions, all in original leatherette-covered attache-style case, ca. 1936, overall excellent condition, the set.. **300**

English Field Camera

Perken, Son & Rayment field camera, mahogany & brass w/original lacquer, half plate, double extension type, original

French Photosphere Camera

"Photosphere" camera, all metal, w/rare magazine back, France, ca. 1890s (ILLUS.)... **2,500-3,500**

Rare French "Photosphere" Camera

"Photosphere" camera, for 9 x 12cm plates, comes w/one dark slide & hard-to-find original viewfinder, rare, France, ca. 1888 (ILLUS.)... **1,996**

Scarce French "Photosphere" Camera

"Photosphere" camera, metal case complete w/original viewfinder, plate holder & focusing screen, France, ca. 1888, excellent condition (ILLUS.) **1,400**

French "Physiograph" Camera

"Physiograph" binocular stereo camera, by Leon Bloch, detective/spy-type, w/45 x 107mm magazine & original binocular case, rare, France, ca. 1896 (ILLUS.).. **2,500**

Koopman All-metal "Presto" Camera

"Presto" Camera, all-metal, by E.B. Koopman, New York, New York, holds four 1 1/4 x 1 1/4" plates, exterior w/nice aged gunmetal patina, some surface rust to internal plate holder, four exposed plates included, ca. 1896 (ILLUS.).............. **800**

Putnam Marvel Camera

Putnam Marvel Camera No. 383, w/brass-barreled Scovill Waterbury lens #112938 w/rotating wheel stops, original wooden box, ca. 1890, 5 x 8" (ILLUS.) **300**

Revere Stereo 33 Camera

All-metal "Presto" Camera

"Presto" camera, all-metal, "E.B. Koopman, New York, Sole Mfr.," model holds four 1 1/4 x 1 1/4" plates, working gravity shutter, original anodized finish, some minor internal rust spots, rare, ca. 1896 (ILLUS.) **950**

Purma Special camera, black Bakelite, the shutter controlled by gravity holding camera either upright or oblong, in original box w/two close-up lenses & yellow filter in original boxes, England, ca. 1930 (ILLUS. bottom of page) **72**

Revere Stereo 33 camera, 35mm, black & silver case w/f3.5 Amaton lens, shutter speeds to 1/200th of a second, MFX synchronization, excellent condition w/original leather case (ILLUS.) **222**

Purma Special Camera

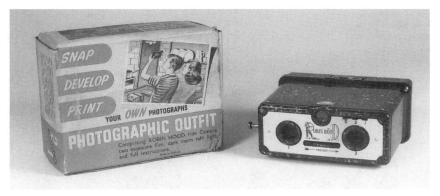

"Robin Hood" Camera Outfit

Ricoh Teleca 240 Camera

Ricoh Teleca 240 camera, half frame 35mm type w/motorized film transport built into 7 x 50 binoculars, w/original shoulder/chest brace, neck strap & instructions in original fitted case, Japan, ca. 1971 (ILLUS.) **600**

"Robin Hood" camera outfit, multicolored Bakelite, in original box containing camera, printing paper, instructions & folding stereoscope, rare (ILLUS. top of page) **175**

Rollei A26 camera, 35mm, black crinkled case, w/C26 flash attachment w/no charger, excellent condition, the set (ILLUS. bottom of page) **60**

Rouch "Eureka" detective camera, quarter-plate model, rectangular

mahogany case w/brass campaign-tropical style corner reinforcements, fully working shutter w/Rouch 5 x 4" brass barreled lens, comes w/seven metal plate holders, completely original, excellent condition, England, ca. 1888 .... **950**

Sanderson Whole Plate Field Camera

Sanderson whole plate field camera, original brass lacquer, w/Thornton Pickard string set, roller blind shutter

Rollei A26 Camera & Flash Attachment

w/Dallmeyer lens, original black bellows, includes one double dark slide, England, ca. 1910 (ILLUS.) **400**

Scott Patent Field Camera Outfit

Scott field camera outfit, by J.T. Chapman, mahogany & brass inlay, maroon bellows, includes camera w/7 x 5" Optimus lens by Perkin, Son & Rayments, pack of Waterhouse stops, Thornton Pickard roller blind shutter & three double dark slides, all in original canvas case, Patent No. 12389, Manchester, England, ca. 1890s (ILLUS.) **550**

"Seneca - Camera City View Camera"

Seneca "Camera City View Camera," for 5 x 7" plates, fully working shutter & f6.3 Enolde Anastigmat lens, Seneca Camera Co., Rochester, New York, ca. 1910 (ILLUS.) **275**

"Seneca" No. 9 Camera

Seneca "No. 9 camera," embossed black leather exterior, double extension folding plate type, w/original Seneca Rapid Convertible 5 x 7" lens, fully operational shutter, original red bellows, Seneca Camera Co., Rochester, New York, ca. 1915 (ILLUS.) **275**

Simda stereo panoramascope camera, France, ca. 1955 (ILLUS. bottom of page, left w/Wollensak camera) **850-1,250**

Sliding box wet plate camera, mahogany, 5" sq. focusing screen, no identifying marks on camera or lens, England, ca. 1860s **2,000**

Rare Early English Camera

Simda & Wollensak Cameras

Sliding box wet plate camera, mahogany, w/Cooke lens, 3 3/4 x 3 3/4" ground glass focusing screen, rare, England, ca. 1865 (ILLUS. previous page) **3,500**

Snappy subminiature camera, 35mm, black & silver case, made in Occupied Japan, ca. 1949, near-mint in worn leather case (ILLUS.) **212**

Sliding Box Wet Plate Camera

Sliding box wet plate camera, wooden case, England, ca. 1855-65 (ILLUS.)
.... **2,000-3,000**

English Sliding Box Camera

Sliding box wet plate camera, wooden case w/dovetailed construction, brass-barreled lens, rack & pinion focusing knob & slit for waterhouse stops, 4 3/4 x 4 3/4" glass focusing screen, England, ca. 1855-60, waterhouse stops not included, ancient repair to side of base board, stains, 6 1/2 x 9 1/4" (ILLUS.) **2,750**

Soho Cadet Camera

Soho Cadet camera, reddish brown Bakelite, matching bellows & face plate, England, ca. 1930 (ILLUS.) **65**

"Sport" German Folding Camera

"Sport" folding camera, 9 x 12cm plate model, marked "Sport - GebrauchsmusterSchutz - No. 1500," simple string pull sector shutter works well, push-pull focusing lens, w/original view finder & matching walnut handle, small age crack on bottom left front, Germany, ca. 1900 (ILLUS.) **800**

Occupied Japan Snappy Mini Camera

1950s Russian Sputnik Stereo Camera

Sputnik stereo camera, rectangular plastic case, shutter works w/speeds from 1/15th to 1/125th of a second, uses 120 roll film, w/original case, Russia, late 1950s, overall . excellent condition (ILLUS.).. **110**

Lumiere "Sterelux" Model I Stereo Camera

"Sterelux" Model I stereo camera, by Lumiere, roll film type, w/f4.5 "Spector" lenses, fully working shutter w/speeds from 1/25 to 1/100 of a second, w/leather carrying case, France, ca. 1920s (ILLUS.).. **130**

Wollensak "Stereo 10" Camera

"Stereo 10" stereoscopic camera, Wollensak, 35 mm type, F2.7 "Amaton"

lenses, fully functional shutter w/speeds from 1/2 to 1/300 of a second, includes lens caps, flash gun & leather case (ILLUS.).. **500**

"Stereo 33" Stereoscopic Camera

"Stereo 33" stereoscopic camera, Revere, 35mm type, F3.5 "Amaton" lenses, fully functional shutter w/speeds from 1/2 to 1/200 of a second, ca. 1953 (ILLUS.).. **150**

"Stereo Cameo" German-made Camera

"Stereo Cameo" camera, made for W. Butcher & Sons, folding-type, fully functional w/five plate holders all in original box w/tape repairs, made in Germany, ca. 1910 (ILLUS.) **225**

Stereo Realist f2.8 Camera

Stereo Realist f2.8 camera, Model ST 1042, w/a pair of sunshade/filter holders & type A filters, fully functioning in ever-ready case, excellent condition, uses standard 35mm film, ca. 1955 (ILLUS.) **350**

Stereo-panoramic camera outfit, drop-front style, rectangular hardwood case w/original dark maroon bellows & a pair of "Symetrique 1/2 Grand Angle" lenses w/stereo shutter, also includes a separate lens panel w/lens & shutter for panoramic photographs, three tambour-style double dark slides, a viewfinder & three leather lens caps, all in original canvas case, internal septum not present, rare outfit, excellent condition, France, ca. 1910 .... **2,750**

Patented George Smith Sciopticon

Stereoscopic camera, marked "George Smith's Sciopticon - Patent no. 3014 - 1881" on a small brass medallion, mahogany case w/brass trim & original dark blue bellows, crank handle for focusing, tilt feature for architectural work, w/an additional single lens panel for mono work, England, late 19th c. (ILLUS.)... **1,700**

Stereoscopic field camera, ivory plaque marked "A. Birnie Maker Dundee," dark hardwood w/original dark maroon square-cut bellows & internal septum, unmarked matched brass lenses w/iris-style diaphragms, w/an additional lens board w/lens for mono work & three double dark slides, all in the original leather case, overall excellent condition, Scotland, ca. 1890s (ILLUS. bottom of page)... **1,800**

Unmarked Stereoscopic Camera

Stereoscopic camera, folds out from rectangular box w/carrying handle, original dark maroon square-cut bellows & internal septum, unmarked but matched brass lenses w/iris-style diaphragms, Thornton Pickard-style shutter works well, w/three double dark slides, England or France, ca. 1900, excellent condition (ILLUS.) **2,500**

Birnie Stereoscopic Field Camera

English Stereoscopic Field Camera

Stereoscopic field camera, mahogany & brass, tailboard style, 5" Wray Stereoscopic lenses consecutively numbered 5082 & 5083, w/septum & lens caps that match maroon leather of bellows, 5 x 7 1/2" focusing screen, tilting back extension for architectural work, ivory plaque reads "The Photographic Artists Stores, 43 Charterhouse Square, London," ca. 1900 (ILLUS.)...................... **1,485**

Stereoscopic Field Camera

Stereoscopic Field camera, wooden case, England, ca. 1880s (ILLUS.)........... **2,000-3,000**

Stereoscopic Tailboard Camera

Stereoscopic Tailboard camera, mahogany & brass w/original lacquer, "Stereoscopic Co. Ltd., 110 & 108 Regent St., & 64 Cheapside," original maroon leather bellows, brass-barreled stereo lenses, removable internal septum for stereo work, additional lens panel w/LSC Rapid Rectilinear lens for mono work, England, ca. 1900 (ILLUS.)... **1,500**

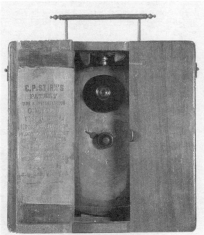

Rare Stirn Concealed Vest Camera No. 1

Stirn Concealed Vest Camera No. 1, fits into shallow square hinged wooden box w/original paper label, signs of light use but overall excellent condition, w/a facsimile Stirn catalog, Stirn Cameras, Germany and New York, ca. 1886 (ILLUS.)... **3,750**

Stirn Concealed Vest Camera

Stirn Concealed Vest Camera No. 1, round nickel plated shape, working shutter, original leather strap, worn original box, Stirn Cameras, Germany and New York, ca. 1886 (ILLUS.) **1,900**

Stirn Concealed Vest Camera No. 1

Stirn Concealed Vest Camera No. 1, round w/anodized brass finish, good aged patina, fine condition, Stirn Cameras, Germany and New York, ca. 1892 (ILLUS.)... **1,500**

Stirn Concealed Vest Camera

Stirn Concealed Vest Camera No. 2, w/unusual leather ever-ready carrying case, both camera & case embossed w/"J. Robinson & Sons, 172 Regent Street, London," Stirn Cameras, Germany and New York, ca. 1888 (ILLUS.).. **2,250**

"Stylophot" Subminiature Camera

"Stylophot" subminiature camera, designed to resemble a fountain pen, three f stops w/single speed shutter, w/original leather case & instructions, France, ca. 1955 (ILLUS. previous page) **178**

TDC Stereo Colorist II 35mm Camera

TDC Stereo Colorist II camera, 35mm, w/f3 1/2 Rodenstock lenses w/shutter speeds from 1/10 to 1/200 of a second, leather carrying case, ca. 1957 (ILLUS.)...... **180**

Telephot Tintype Button Camera

Telephot Tintype Button camera, by British Ferrotype Co., nickel plated,

10 3/4" l. barrel, ca. 1910, plating pitted (ILLUS.) **750**

English "Binocular Camera"

"The Binocular Camera," No. 1 size for 1 1/2 & 2 1/2" plates, one lens used as viewfinder, the other as taking lens, w/12 internal plate holders & original leather case, The London Stereoscopic Co., ca. 1898 (ILLUS.).. **302**

"The Duchess" Field Camera

Thornton Pickard "Stereo Puck" Camera

"The Duchess" half-plate field camera & outfit, mahogany & brass w/ivory label, w/a rapid rectilinear lens w/a slot for Waterhouse stops, original maroon bellows, figured brass w/original lacquer, outfit includes three double dark slides numbered 1 to 6, a set of Waterhouse stops, an unusual early viewfinder & a tripod, all in worn original fitted leather case, England, ca. 1890s, the group (ILLUS.) **450**

"The Royalty Stereoscopic" camera, by Joshua Billcliff, Manchester, England, grained mahogany case w/brass hood, consecutively numbered Plaubel Doppel Orthar lenses, original internal septum & dark maroon bellows, w/one double dark slide, excellent condition, ca. 1890s **1,800**

Thornton Pickard "Stereo Puck" camera, low rectangular black case, complete w/viewer, instructions, sample stereo views & original box, England, ca. 1925, mint condition (ILLUS. bottom of previous page) **425**

Thornton Pickard "Stereo Puck" camera, w/a Stereo Puck Viewer, both in original boxes, excellent condition, the set (camera box lid missing) **180**

Tintype Button Camera

Tintype button camera, metal, ca. 1900 (ILLUS.) **1,000-1,500**

Tisdell & Whittelsey Detective Camera

Tisdell & Whittelsey detective camera, black leather-covered case numbered 356, unusual model for 4 x 5" plates, marked lens & internal tapered cloth-covered bellows, w/the original five plate holders, internal focusing screen, five Waterhouse stops & detachable internal viewfinder, in fitted box w/replaced top handle, United States, box measures 7 x 12 1/2", 7" h., ... **1,300**

"Tone" Subminiature Camera

"Tone" subminiature camera, w/original leather case, ca. 1948 (ILLUS.) **145**

Toyoca 16 subminiature camera, in original box w/miniature tripod & roll of film, Japan, ca. 1955 (ILLUS. left w/miniature cameras).................................... **135**

TransWorld Airlines novelty camera, printed metal in the shape of a bulbous four-engine jet liner, mint condition in original bag **110**

"ULCA" Subminiature Camera

"ULCA" subminiature camera, original black enamel paint, United States, ca. 1935 (ILLUS.)... **65**

"Verascope F40" Stereo Camera

"Verascope F40" stereo camera, by Jules Richard for Busch Camera Company of Chicago, 35mm type, w/supplementary Steinhell 12.5mm "Redufocus" for super wide angle work, f3.5 Berthiot lenses, fully working shutter w/speeds from 1 to 1/250 of a second, France, 1950s (ILLUS.)... **1,900**

Houghton Victo Folding Camera

Victo camera, by Houghton, folding-type, mahogany & brass half-plate model, Thornton Pickard roller blind shutter works well, w/an f4.5 Aldis Uno Anastigmat lens, w/two double dark slides & the original black focusing dark cloth, all in the canvas case, overall excellent condition, England, ca. 1900 (ILLUS.)... **325**

Videon II Stereo Camera

Videon II stereo camera, 35mm type, F3.5 Ilex "Stereon" lenses, fully working shutter, speeds from 1/10 to 1/100 of a second, w/leather case (ILLUS.)................. **250**

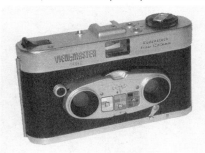

View-Master Stereo Mark II Camera

View-Master Stereo Mark II color camera, 35mm type, F2.8 Rodenstock "Trinar" lenses, fully working shutter & integral

Warwick No. 2 Box Camera & Box

exposure calculator, w/case w/detached flap, ca. 1960s (ILLUS. previous page) **120**

Warwick No. 2 box camera, black crinkled leatherette case, near mint in original box, England, ca. 1930s (ILLUS. bottom of previous page) **28**

Waterbury Stereo View Camera

Waterbury stereo camera, 5 x 8" view-type, Model No. 398, w/a matched pair of Waterbury lenses & a Scovill & Adams lens for mono work, mounted on an unnumbered lens panel, also w/a dark slide, no internal septum, good used condition, United States, ca. 1885 (ILLUS.) **800**

Watson detective camera, a quarter-plate wooden camera w/dark maroon square-cut bellows & a Watson 5 x 4 R.R. lens, shutter works well, in a black leather-covered box w/a hinged top w/additional double dark slides numbered 1 to 6, camera excellent condition, Watson & Sons, England, ca. 1890 (ILLUS. following) **1,100**

Watson Detective Camera in Box

Watson field camera outfit, half-plate type, mahogany & brass, burgundy bellows, Grubb "Aplanatic Doublet" lens No. 5254, five Waterhouse stops in leather case, three double dark slides, all in fitted leather case w/Watson label on interior, also includes hard-to-find "Eastman Kodak Co." roll film back w/patent date of May 5, 1885 designed to fit camera, Watson & Sons, England (ILLUS. bottom of page) **1,815**

Watson Field Camera Outfit Label

"Watson & Sons" Field Camera Outfit

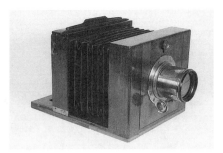

Rare English 1870s Wet Plate Camera

Wet plate sliding box camera, by C.E. Clifford, London, England, fine hardwood closed box case w/brass lens, focusing screen shows an image 7 1/2" sq., original lacquered lens w/some tarnish, overall excellent condition, includes an early printing frame, ca. 1860, case 8 x 9 1/2", 9 1/2" h.................................... **3,750**

Watson Field Camera Outfit

Watson field camera outfit, mahogany & brass, original maroon bellows, Watson 10 x 8" brass-barreled f8 lens, original Watson leather case w/label containing three 10 x 8 double dark slides, Watson & Sons, England, ca. 1900 (ILLUS. also on previous page) **700**

Rare Wet Plate Sliding Box Camera

Wet plate sliding box camera, walnut case w/quality dovetailing, brass barreled lens w/brass lens cap & a rack & pinion focus, also a removable focusing ground glass screen, England or France, ca. 1850s, base 7 1/2 x 8 3/4" (ILLUS.)...................... **4,750**

Watson & Sons Stereoscopic Camera

Watson stereoscopic camera, mahogany & brass, rack & pinion focusing, tilting back, brass-barreled J.H. Dallmeyer lenses, rotating wheel stops consecutively numbered 14110 & 14111, maroon bellows, marked "Watson & Sons, 515 High Holborn, London," ca. 1885 (ILLUS.).. **2,500**

Wet plate camera, mahogany & brass, tailboard style, 5 x 6 1/2" focusing screen, dark maroon bellows, no identifying marks on camera or lens, rare, England, ca. 1870s (ILLUS. following) **1,452**

Wollensak Model 10 Stereo Camera

Wollensak Model 10 stereo camera, w/f2.7 lens & speeds to 1/30 of a second, one of the best 35mm stereo cameras, mint in box w/instructions, 1950s (ILLUS. previous page) **950**

Wollensak Model 10 stereoscopic camera, America, ca. 1955 (ILLUS. right w/Simda camera) **450-650**

buttons, shutter may not work due to missing pneumatic squeeze bulb, excellent appearance, ca. 1909 (ILLUS.).. **1,300**

Zeiss Contessa-nettel "Ergo" Camera

Zeiss Contessa-nettel "Ergo" camera, spy type, painted black, made to look like a monocular but actually takes photograph at right angles, scarce, Germany, ca. 1927 (ILLUS.) **1,240**

"Wonder Photo Cannon"

"Wonder Photo Cannon" camera, by the Chicago Ferrotype Co., cannon-shaped metal case, for making 1" tintype photo

CHAPTER 2
Camera Accessories

"Agfa Amateur Flashlight Outfit"

"Agfa Amateur Flashlight Outfit," rectangular metal flash pan w/turned wood handle, flash coil & instructions, w/original box, excellent condition (ILLUS.).. $144

"Agfa Flashlight Lamp," in original box, complete w/instructions, measuring spoon & "sparking material" (ILLUS. bottom of page) 100

Camera exposure meter, pocket watch-style, w/four different dials, Germany, excellent condition in original box (ILLUS. top of next page) **137**

Early Brass Lens

Daguerreian/wet plate era lens No. 10,450, by C.C. Harrison, New York, brass, focal length of 12", includes

"Agfa Flashlight Lamp"

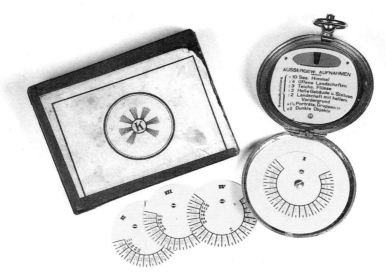

German Pocket Watch-style Exposure Meter

leather lens cap & three Waterhouse stops, mid-barrel & rack & pinion focusing knob are replacements, 8" l. (ILLUS.)... **200**

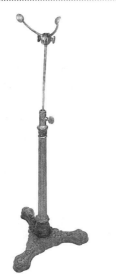

Rare Daguerrian Studio Head Brace

Daguerrian-collodian era studio head brace, cast iron w/tall adjustable rod, few very minor rush marks, rare early piece, mid-19th c., extends from 36" to 48" h. (ILLUS.).. **1,722**

"Luxol" Darkroom Lamp

Darkroom lamp, "Luxol" model, England, ca. 1900, w/original canister, excellent condition, lamp 4" h. (ILLUS.)......... **70**

Kodak Darkroom Lantern

Darkroom lantern, metal lamp on low cylindrical font base, front flap embossed "Kodak," excellent condition, ca. 1930s (ILLUS. previous page) **25**

Early Darkroom Safe Light

Darkroom safe light, Carbutt style, w/original illuminant, all glasswork appears original, "P" on front louvered door, America, part of interior glass chimney missing, ca. 1870s-80s (ILLUS.) **275**

Darkroom Safe Light

Darkroom safe light, ruby colored, marked "ICA, Dresden," early 20th c. (ILLUS.) **425**

Developing Tank

Developing tank, Eastman Kodak, nickel plated, for 5 x 7" plates, w/interior plate holders (ILLUS.) **55**

"Diaphot" exposure meter, by Zeiss Ikon, pocket watch-shaped, in original leather case, excellent condition, Germany **65**

"Eastman Flash Cartridge No. 2" Tin

"Eastman Flash Cartridge No. 2," in original cylindrical tin containing one cartridge & instructions, ca. 1890s (ILLUS.) **83**

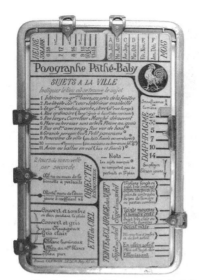

"Posographe Pathe-Baby" Exposure Calculator

Exposure calculator, "Posographe Pathe-Baby" by Kaufman, in original red case, ca. 1920s (ILLUS.)................................ **75**

"Photmetre" Exposure Meter

Exposure meter, brass, "Photmetre" by J. Decoudun, in original box, Paris, France, ca. 1900 (ILLUS.)............................ **125**

Exposure Meter

Exposure meter, original lacquered brass, Watkins & Sons, England, ca. 1880, 1 1/2" d., 2 1/2" h. (ILLUS.) **220**

Watkins Bee Exposure Meter

Exposure meter, Watkins "Bee" Meter, pocket watch-style, w/instructions in original box, excellent condition, ca. 1900 (ILLUS.).. **75**

"Express Daylight Enlarger"

"Express Daylight Enlarger," for 1/4 plates, portable, folds flat for transporting, w/red "bellows," England, ca. 1890 (ILLUS.)......................... **275**

Flash device, "L'Etincelle," cylindrical brass body, for night photography, using pulverized magnesium powder, w/instructions in French in the original box, overall excellent condition, ca. 1890 (ILLUS. top of next page)............................ **325**

French "L'Etincelle" Flash Device

French "Lampe Soleil" Flash Device

Flash device, "Lampe Soleil," short cylindrical brass box w/original lacquer finish, w/instructions in French & original worn box, France, ca. 1890s (ILLUS.) **325**

"Gios Aktinometer" Exposure Meter

"Gios Aktinometer" exposure meter, cylindrical metal shape, probably German, ca. 1940s, very good condition, 3 3/4" h. (ILLUS.) **10**

Guerry Double Flap-style Shutter

Guerry double flap-style shutter, France, ca. 1888, 3 1/4 x 3 1/2 x 1 3/4" (ILLUS.).. **110**

Rare Hume Double Guillotine-style Shutter

Guillotine-style Shutter

"ICA" Watch-style Exposure Meter

Guillotine-style shutter, for mounting over a 2" d. lens, using different rubber bands varies speed of shutter, United States (ILLUS.).. 250

"Haka" exposure meter, metal disk-shaped, some wear to dial but overall excellent condition, w/original leather pouch, France 75

"Heydes Aktino Photo Meter," metal disk-shaped, in original aluminum case, excellent condition... 65

Hume double guillotine-style shutter, mahogany & brass, brass w/original lacquer, marked "Wm. Hume, Edinburgh - Patent Applied For," tiny crack in front of wood, excellent condition, 19th c. (ILLUS. top of page) 225

"ICA" exposure meter, round pocket watch-style, w/instructions & original leather case, Germany, excellent condition (ILLUS.) 50

Kaufmann's "Le Posograph" exposure calculator, detailed rectangular design in a metal frame, w/original leather pouch, excellent condition, France (ILLUS. top of next page)............................. 100

Kodak filter set, three-piece, nicely cased, ca. 1920, excellent condition (ILLUS. bottom of next page, left w/Premo lens accessories) 40

Kaufmann's
"Le Posograph"
Exposure Calculator

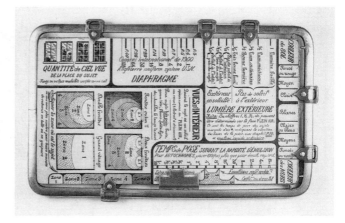

Lancaster Patent "Instantograph" shutter, brass, fits lens of approximately 1 5/8" d. interior, screw thread, works on rubber band principal, using different sizes of rubber bands to vary shutter speeds, J. Lancaster, England (ILLUS.) **250**

Lancaster Patent "Instantograph" shutter, round metal disk w/screw thread, fits lens of about 1 5/8" interior diameter, works on a simple rubber band principal using different sized rubber bands to vary the shutter speeds, fully working, excellent condition, J. Lancaster, England **180**

Lancaster Patent "Instantograph" shutter, round metal disk w/screw thread, fits lens of about 1 5/8" interior diameter, works on a spring principal, the shutter speed changed by tightening a simple tension brake operated by a thumbscrew, J. Lancaster, England **225**

Lancaster Patent Shutter

Kodak Filter Set & Premo Lens Accessories

Lancaster "Instantograph" Shutter

Lancaster Patent "Instantograph" shutter, to fit a lens of 1/8" d., screw thread, brass a little dull, J. Lancaster, England (ILLUS.)... **120**

Negative Safe

Negative safe, Rochester Optical Co., black leather covered wood, suitable for glass negatives, autochromes (ILLUS.) **70**

Scarce Child's Photo Studio Head Stand

Photo studio head stand, child-sized, cast iron tripod base centered by an adjustable rod, probably from the late wet plate period, ca. 1870s-80s, a few rust spots, extended 33" h. (ILLUS.) **450**

Portable photographer's developing tent-changing bag, patented by W.R. Baker, December 22, 1890, Patent No. 20864, sold as "The Tourists Developing Tent," completely folds up into a portable mahogany box w/brass carrying handle, drawer at bottom contains integral zinc-lined developing tray, few dings on box exterior, overall excellent condition, very rare, box 12 1/4" sq., 3 1/2" h. (ILLUS. bottom of page) **1,300**

Rare Photographer's Portable Tent

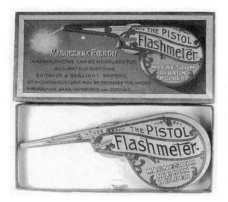

"Pistol Flashmeter" Ribbon

Ribbon, magnesium, "Pistol Flashmeter," in original box, ca. 1900 (ILLUS.)....................... **85**

Rochester "Premo" camera lens accessories, includes yellow filter, copying lens, wide angle lens, telephoto lens, duplicator lens & portrait lens, in original leather case, the set (ILLUS. right w/Kodak filter set)... **70**

"Salmon's Patent Adjustable Vignetter"
Darkroom Accessory

"Salmon's Patent Adjustable Vignetter," darkroom accessory, in original box w/instructions, ca. 1900 (ILLUS.) **30**

Three Brass Lenses in Fitted Case

Set of brass lenses, a 210mm Hermagis, a "Aplanstigmat" w/a Tele-Objective converter lens & a Vulga 13 x 18 "Grand Angle" lens, all in a fitted box & each retaining original lacquer, the Hermagis w/some balsaming & no flanges, ca. 1890s, the set (ILLUS.) **450**

1937 Paris World's Fair Photo Viewer

Souvenir photograph viewer, from the Paris World's Fair of 1937, contains 18 real photos of the various buildings on a continuous roll, excellent condition, 2 1/4 x 4" (ILLUS.)... **150**

Close-up Lens for Mikroma Camera

Stereo Mikroma camera close-up lens, 1-0.6 meter (ILLUS.) **45**

Stereo-Redufocus Lens Attachment

Stereo-Redufocus attachment, wide angle (25mm) lens attachment for the Stereo Realist camera, will fit either the f2.8 or f3.5 Realist Camera, w/original leather case, excellent condition (ILLUS.) **360**

"Stop Watch Meter," by Adams & Co., pocket watch-form, combination type w/a conventional Wynne's type "Infallible" meter on one side w/a Swiss-made stop watch on the other, silver plate case tarnished, working condition, overall excellent condition, ca. 1911 .... **475**

Actual Photo Studio "Birdie" Prop

Studio distracting device, figural "birdie," stylized metal bird atop a rubber tube above a rounded base to hold water, blowing through tube makes a bird sound & moves the tail, late 19th - early 20th c. (ILLUS.) **350**

"The Phantom Shutter"

"The Phantom Shutter," flap-type, rectangular wooden framework, appears to be a variant of the Branson Phoenix Shutter, England, ca. 1884 (ILLUS.) **275**

Pickard Patent Roller Blind Shutter

Thornton Pickard patent roller blind shutter, made to fit over a lens approximately 1 3/4" d., working, England, ca. 1900 (ILLUS.) **110**

Voightlander & Sohn Brass Barrel Lens

Thornton Pickard Shutter

Thornton Pickard roller blind, string set shutter, for mounting over a 2" d. lens, England (ILLUS.)... **175**

ViewMaster 36" Close-up Attachment

ViewMaster 36" close-up lens attachment, for the ViewMaster "Personal" Stereo Camera, excellent condition w/original leather case (ILLUS.) **160**

Voightlander & Sohn lens No. 10861, 6" (15cm) long, brass barrel-style, focal length of 56" (14cm), rack & pinion focusing, some original lacquer, w/a slit for Waterhouse stops, mounting flange cut off at some point to mount on a camera (ILLUS. top of page, left) **95**

Voightlander & Sohn lens No. 25148, 4 3/4" (12cm) long, brass barrel-style w/fixed focus, focus length of 18" (43cms), slit for Waterhouse stops, length suggests use as a portrait lens, overall very good condition (ILLUS. top of page, right) **45**

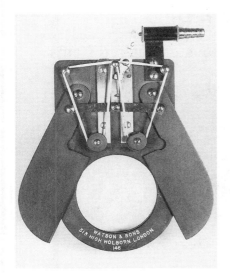

"Flying Wing"-style Shutter

Watson & Sons "flying wing"-style shutter, from Watson Camera outfit, marked "Watson & Sons - 313 High Holborn London - 146," ca. 1880s (ILLUS.).. **515**

"Wynne's Infallible Exposure Meter," classic pocket watch-style, in original tin box, England, excellent condition (ILLUS. following).. **85**

"Wynne's Infallible Exposure Meter," later pocket watch-style, w/original leather pouch, tin box, paper & instructions, excellent condition (ILLUS. bottom of page)... **150**

"Wynne's Infallible Exposure Meter"

"Wynne's Infallible Hunter Meter"

"Wynne's Infallible Hunter Meter," pocket watch-style, in original tin box, excellent condition, England, ca. 1933 (ILLUS.) **75**

"Wynne's Infallible Hunter Meter" with Box

CHAPTER 3
Magic Lanterns, Optical Toys & Related Items

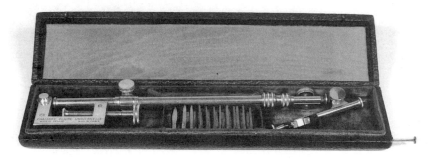

Chambre Claire Universelle Camera Lucida in Box

Unusual Advertising "Animatiscope"

"Animatiscope" flicker toy, advertising-type, an upright embossed & printed paper box w/side crank handle, titled "Ballet Dance," advertising on side for H.T. Moss, Clothing, Hats and Furnishing, patented October 12, 1897, sides somewhat soiled, scarce, 1 x 3", 3" h. (ILLUS.) .. **$275**

Camera Lucida, cased, nickel-plated metal, marked "Chambre Claire Universelle," by P. Berville, Paris, France, complete & original in all respects, includes twelve supplementary lenses & instructions, slight wear on exterior of case, overall excellent condition, France, ca. 1900 .... **600**

Camera Lucida, "Chambre Claire Universelle," includes 12 supplementary lenses, in case, France, ca. 1890 (ILLUS. top of page) **250**

Chambre Claire Universelle Camera Lucida

Camera Lucida, "Chambre Claire Universelle," nickel plated, complete & original, comes w/12 supplementary lenses & photocopy of instructions in case, France, ca. 1900 (ILLUS.)............................ **450**

Camera Obscura, toy-size, black metal rectangular box, brass barreled lens pulls in & out to focus image on a ground glass screen, probably German, ca. 1895, 5 x 5 3/4", 4 3/4" h. (some paint wear)......... **250**

Early Toy Camera Obscura

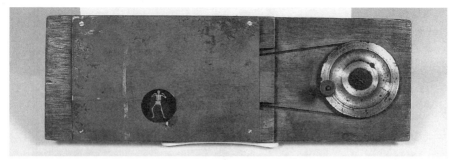

Dancing Skeleton" Choreutoscope

Camera Obscura, toy-size, rectangular red metal case, probably German or French, excellent condition, ca. 1890, 4" x 6", 4" h. (ILLUS. previous page) **300**

Choreutoscope, "Dancing Skeleton," single-pulley mechanical slide w/rotating shutter giving effect of dancing skeleton, should more accurately be referred to as a projecting Phenakistoscope, similar to Ross Wheel of Life, some age to wooden part of slide, ca. 1860s, 4 x 11 1/4" (ILLUS. top of page) **2,094**

"Cinepoli" Optical Toy/Projector

"Cinepoli" optical toy/projector, in original box w/instructions, five "films" & original screen, Italy, ca. 1930s (ILLUS.) **200**

French Combination Viewer

Combination carte de visite mechanical viewer w/stereoscopic front, France, ca. 1870s (ILLUS.) **1,500-2,500**

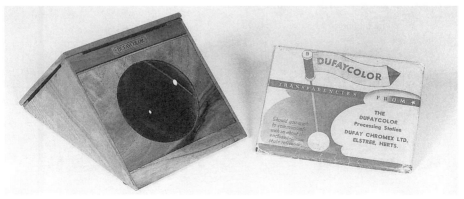

Dufaycolor Viewer

Rare "Fantascope" Set

Dufaycolor viewer, walnut, designed for viewing Dufaycolor transparencies (similar to Diascope used for viewing autochromes), 3 1/2" d. magnifying lens, comes w/original blue filter for viewing in artificial light & a packet of four Dufaycolor transparencies (ILLUS. previous page) **220**

"Fantascope" set, by Ackerman of London, the set composed of 12 animation discs along w/the original wood & ivory handle, all in the original wooden box, discs are very fresh & colorful in overall excellent condition, ca. 1833, England, each disc about 9 3/4" d., case 10 3/4" sq., 1 3/4" h. (ILLUS. top of page) **4,500**

"Filoscope" of Pope Leo XIII

"Filoscope" & Flip Book Optical Toys

"Filoscope" flick-book toy, features images of Pope Leo XIII, a few images creased but overall excellent condition, rare variant, ca. 1900 (ILLUS.).................... **450**

"Filoscope" optical toy, operates on flip book principal, this one showing soldiers boarding a ship, manufactured by The British Mutoscope & Biograph Co., Ltd., rare in this condition, ca. 1910 (ILLUS. bottom of previous page, left w/flip book) **585**

Flip-book, Castrol Oil premium, cover reads "See Sir Malcolm Campbell breaking the world's water speed record," at the top instructions read "Place thumb here and flick," corners worn, ca. 1930s (ILLUS. right w/"Filoscope") **55**

Flip-book, double-sided, titled "Swimming American Girl Champions - Flicker No. 15 - High Dives" (some wear to corners) **60**

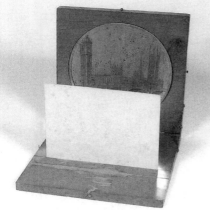

Folding Viewing Device

Folding viewing device, w/concave mirror to give pseudo-stereoscopic effect, 6" d. mirror, for viewing CDVs & other photographs, comes w/12 litho prints of scenes in & around London, ca. 1890s, some silver loss to mirror, 7 1/4" sq., 1" h. closed (ILLUS.)... **45**

"Gramophone-Cinema (The Kinephone)" optical toy, cross between a Zoetrope & a Phenakistascope, discs being placed upon the turntable of a gramophone, a slotted drum then placed on the disc, in original box w/four animated discs, including Felix the Cat, England, ca. 1920s, some rust to wheels that revolve the drum but works well (ILLUS. bottom of page)... **221**

Leatherette-covered Graphoscope

Graphoscope, covered in blue leatherette material, 3 1/2" d. magnifying glass, suitable for cartes de visite, cabinet cards & postcards, 6 x 6", 1 1/4" h. closed (ILLUS.)... **75**

"Gramophone-Cinema (The Kinephone)" Optical Toy

Very Rare "Gyrating Shadow Lantern"

"Gyrating Shadow Lantern" optical toy, McLoughlin Bros., New York, New York, patented October 19, 1875, the lantern w/four fabric-covered panels each decorated w/a different scene, the interior consists of a hot air carousel to which is attached a variety of amusing cut-out figures, together w/two adjustable candle-holders, heat from the candles sets the carousel in motion & ghostly images of silhouetted figures float by, lantern stands 10 1/2 x 12 1/2" on a footed wooden base & folds neatly into a 12 1/2 x 14" original box w/colorfully lithographed label, very rare, some professional restoration on box, some figures w/damage or missing parts, the set (ILLUS.) **4,250**

Home eye testing device, wood & cardboard, legend indicating "Made in U.S.A., property of Self Test Optical Company, Toronto, Ontario," probably 1930s, 11 1/2" l. (ILLUS. bottom of page) **55**

"Home Town Movie Theatre" optical toy, tinplate, Louis Marx & Co., New York, the knobs on the side revolving various cartoon scenes of "Bobby and Betty's Trip to Jungleland," ca. 1930s, some wear spots

to paint, 3 1/2 x 5", 2 1/4" h. (ILLUS. top of next page) **45**

"Jollyfilm" Viewer in Box with Loop

"Jollyfilm" handheld viewer, plastic, for 8mm loops, w/one loop of saloon brawl, in original box, 1950s (ILLUS.) **75**

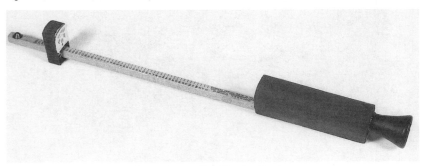

Optical Home Eye Testing Device

Marx "Home Town Movie Theatre"

Kaleidoscope, brass barrel-type, revolving cell appears to have original contents, including oil-filled ampoules, w/a slide that enables the objective lens to move back & forth, very minor pitting & tarnish, overall excellent condition, ca. 1880-90 (ILLUS.) **550**

Kaleidoscope, brass cylindrical type, bright & clear image, brass lacquer tarnished, late 19th c. (ILLUS. top of next page) **300**

Kaleidoscope on Brass Stand

Kaleidoscope, brass, on brass stand, ca. 1900, 7 1/2" l. barrel, 11" h. (ILLUS.) **1,000**

Early Brass Barrel Kaleidoscope

Victorian Brass Kaleidoscope

Brewster Telescoping Kaleidoscope

Brass-barreled English Kaleidoscope

Kaleidoscope, brass-barreled, removable cell for changing contents, England, ca. 1890, 6 3/4" l. barrel (ILLUS.) **350**

Kaleidoscope, Brewster patent telescoping model, objective lens marked "J. Ruthven, Edinburgh," the official maker & seller for Brewster Patent Kaleidoscope for Edinburgh, 6 1/2" l. scope extends to 10" l., comes w/four cells & photocopy of original instructions dated 1818, the kaleidoscope & four cells each contained in what appears to be their original cardboard tubes, rare, one cell has missing glass (ILLUS.) **7,000**

Scarce Bush Kaleidoscope & Stand

Kaleidoscope, Bush Patent type, black metal cylinder w/shiny metal lens end, raised on a finely turned wood replacement stand, barrel in excellent condition, ca. 1870s, overall 14" h. (ILLUS.) **600**

Bush Patent Kaleidoscope

Kaleidoscope, C.G. Bush Patent type, black cylindrical tube mounted on a turned walnut pedestal base, dated November 14, 1874, excellent condition (ILLUS.) **800**

Kaleidoscope, cylindrical tube covered in red-embossed paper w/gold foil decoration, nickel plate trim w/slight pitting, France, ca. 1890s, excellent condition, 9" l. **484**

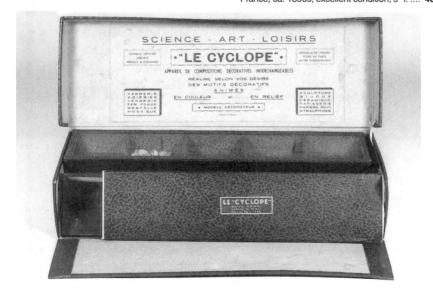

French "Le Cyclope" Kaleidoscope

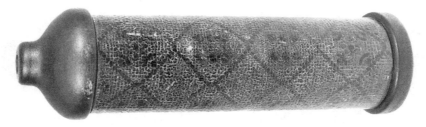

American 1930s Kaleidoscope

Miniature Pocket Kaleidoscope

English "Student's Kaleidoscope"

Kaleidoscope, "Le Cyclope," comes w/instructions in French & original box w/an interior box w/five compartments to hold various objects to be inserted into the Kaleidoscope, France, ca. 1946, excellent condition, 12" l. (ILLUS.) 310

Kaleidoscope, metal & decorated cardboard cylinder, probably American, ca. 1930s, excellent condition, 10" l. (ILLUS. top of page) 137

Kaleidoscope, miniature pocket-type, brass, marked "Van Cort," 5 1/4" l. (ILLUS. middle photo) 75

Kaleidoscope, "Student's Kaleidoscope," metal cylinder w/a black crinkle finish raised & adjusting on a post above the base, Signalling Equipment, Ltd., England, w/original box, ca. 1940s (ILLUS. bottom photo) 250

Kaleidoscope, tapering decorative paper tube, couple of minor stains, late 19th c., probably English, very good condition, 11" l. (ILLUS. top of next page) 272

Kaleidoscope on pedestal base, smaller cylindrical size in blue faux snake skin material raised on a turned wood stand, overall excellent condition, probably late 19th - early 20th c., barrel 7 1/4" l., overall 9" h. (tiny solder repair to brass bracket holding the scope on the stand) 375

Kaleidoscopic color top or optical wheel toy, metal, 6" d. wheel where various multicolored discs are placed, when spun it gives a kaleidoscopic effect, a wooden handle fits in a square base, w/five hand-painted discs, all contained in original mahogany box, very slight wear to center of discs, overall excellent condition, very rare, ca. 1860-70, the set 850

Decorative Paper Tube Victorian Kaleidoscope

Rare Kaleidoscopic Color Top Toy

Kaleidoscopic color top toy, by Elliott Brothers, London, apparently complete w/ disks & wooden holder in original wooden box, some soil on a few disks, overall excellent condition, ca. 1860, rare (ILLUS.)..... **1,500**

Kinora animation viewer, deluxe miniature version of Mutoscope, light colored satinwood w/banded inlay, comes w/six reels including one of the Coronation of King Edward VII, very smooth crank movement, overall excellent condition, The Kinora Company, Ltd., London, England, ca. 1912, base 6 x 12", the set .. **2,250**

ture, shaped long satinwood base w/banded inlay, platform base w/angled viewer, crank handle turns the reel & shows a series of photographs creating an animation effect based in the flickerbook, metal viewing hood w/slight wear, w/two animation reels, "Zebras at the Zoo" & #73 (youths being tossed in a blanket), The Kinora Company, Ltd., London, England, ca. 1912 (ILLUS.)........ **2,000**

Deluxe Version of Kinora Viewer

Kinora animation viewer, deluxe version, mahogany, based on the flicker book principal, w/crank winding movement, comes w/three real photograph reels, The Kinora Company, Ltd., London, England, ca. 1910, 6 3/4 x 13 1/2", 11" h. (ILLUS.).......... **2,750**

Deluxe Kinora Animation Viewer

Kinora animation viewer, deluxe model, home version of a Mutoscope in minia-

Kinora Oak Hand-crank Reel Viewer

Kinora hand-crank viewer, The Kinora Company, Ltd., London, golden oak, machines work on similar principal to a Mutoscope, reels could either be purchased or rented, crank-operated, w/two reels, "Tobogganing" & "Pillow Fight," introduced in 1908, The Kinora Company, Ltd., London, England, overall excellent condition (ILLUS.) **2,000**

Early "Magic Disk" Phenakistascope

"Le Phenakisticope" optical toy, magic animation disk toy, boxed set apparently complete w/eight double-sided animated disks plus one slotted viewing disk, box w/an internal mirror used for viewing disks, disks somewhat soiled, box worn w/carefully repaired hinge, box label darkened, ca. 1850 (ILLUS.) **2,500**

Kinora Motion Picture Viewer

Kinora motion picture viewer, The Kinora Company, Ltd., London, England, ca. 1900 (ILLUS.) **2,000-2,500**

Kinora viewer on pedestal base, double model, mahogany, w/two sets of lenses to enable two people to view at the same time, a home version of a Mutoscope in miniature based on a flicker-book principal, overall excellent condition w/smooth crank movement, w/seven various reels, The Kinora Company, Ltd., London, England, ca. 1910, base 7" sq., overall 12 1/2" h. **7,250**

Lantern slide projector, lens by Bausch & Lomb, w/bellows, Keystone View Company, United States, ca. 1920s (ILLUS. bottom of page) **149**

"Le Phenakisticope" optical toy, magic animation disk toy, boxed set apparently complete w/twelve animated disks plus one slotted viewing disk w/wooden handle, some discs w/some soil & minor wear, very rare set, France, ca. 1840, the set (ILLUS. top of next page) **3,750**

Magic lantern, all nickel-plate finish, marked "Union Lanterna Magica - Duets. Muster Schutz - Gestetzl Geschutzt," original illuminant & interior glass chimney, Germany, late 19th c. **1,300**

Keystone Lantern Slide Projector

Rare "Le Phenakisticope" Optical Toy

Unusual All-brass Magic Lantern

Magic lantern, all-brass w/thin rectangular base supporting a tapering pedestal & spherical body w/a replaced cylindrical chimney, ca. 1900, 14" h. (ILLUS.) **425**

Magic lantern, biunial-type, mahogany & brass, black japanned chimney, w/original limelights & dissolving valves, England, ca. 1890, 25" h. **4,000**

Art Nouveau Magic Lantern

Magic lantern, brass, Art Nouveau style, ca. 1900 (ILLUS.) **400-600**

Rare Early American Magic Lantern

Magic lantern, by Benjamin Pike & Son, New York, New York, tall rectangular tin-plate form on small paw feet, original black japanned paint w/gilt scroll trim, tall arched chimney, paint scorched off chimney, illuminant missing, overall excellent condition, ca. 1860s, 27" h. (ILLUS.) **726**

Ernst Plank Magic Lantern

Magic lantern, by Ernst Plank, gunmetal grey w/brass, original illuminant, interior glass chimney & box, comes w/19 colorful multiple image strip slides, Germany, ca. 1890, 14" h. (ILLUS.) **456**

Magic lantern, by Ernst Plank, light blue metal upright oval body on small tab feet, tall curved top chimney, gilt-edged high-

lights, illuminant missing, scarce, ca. 1880 (some rust staining) **250**

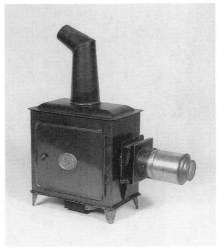

Metal German Magic Lantern

Magic lantern, by Ernst Plank, upright rectangular gunmetal grey case w/original oil illuminant, excellent condition, ca. 1900, Germany, 12" h. (ILLUS.) **125**

George Carette Magic Lantern

Magic lantern, by George Carette, red metal case, w/illuminant, in original box, comes w/box of 12 strip slides, Germany, ca. 1890, 11" h. (ILLUS.) **128**

Magic lantern, by George Carette, thin rectangular base w/panel supports holding the horizontal red metal cylindrical body above the burner, tall tapering cylindrical top chimney, original burner w/glass chimney, overall very good condition, Germany, ca. 1895, 9" h. (some paint wear) **250**

Magic lantern, by Jean Schoenner, all-brass, round pedestal base supporting the spherical body w/a tall cylindrical chimney, in original display box w/nine of the original strip slides, very good condition, Germany, ca. 1880, overall 11 1/2" h. (some black paint missing on front support) **650**

Jean Schoenner German Magic Lantern

Magic lantern, by Jean Schoenner, gun-metal grey metal case w/silvered tin trim, w/original oil illuminant & interior glass chimney, all in original box, w/24 multi-image slides, Germany, ca. 1879, 14" h. (ILLUS.) **450**

"Jubilee Grand Bavaria" Magic Lantern

Magic lantern, by Jean Schoenner, marked "The Jubilee Grand Bavaria," greyish black metal upright cylindrical frame, some rust spots, electrified in the past, w/two glass slides, Germany, ca. 1895, 12" h. (ILLUS.) **225**

Magic lantern, by Jean Schoenner, w/original oil burner, metal case in brilliant red color, Germany, ca. 1880, 15" h. **825**

Magic lantern, by Max Danhorn, upright cylindrical red-painted case w/brass trim, original illuminant & interior glass chim-

ney, overall excellent condition, Germany, ca. 1885, 15" h. (one small ding on domed brass collar) **650**

T.H. McAllister Magic Lantern

Magic lantern, by T.H. McAllister, nickel plate, brass plaque on rear of lamp housing indicates patent date of April 6, 1886, comes w/original tin carrying/storage box, missing lid, scarce, New York, corner wear to bellows, minor rust spots to iron lamp housing & chimney, illuminant not present, 16" l., 19" h. w/telescoping chimney extended (ILLUS.) **665**

Magic lantern, "Delineascope," by Spencer Lens Co., Buffalo, New York, long horizontal black metal case w/extendable lens, fully operational, like-new in original box, ca. 1920s-30s (ILLUS. top of next page) **180**

"Ideal" Magic Lantern

Magic lantern, "Ideal" model, by the Perry Mason Company, complete w/burner & interior chimney w/condenser, black paint, Boston, Massachusetts, ca. 1900, 9" h. (ILLUS.) **110**

"Delineascope" Lantern Slide Projector

"Ideal" or "Gem" Magic Lantern

Magic lantern, "Ideal" or "Gem" model, cylindrical tinplate designs w/black japanning, w/original burner & interior chimney, made exclusively for "Youth's Companion" magazine & used as a premium, United States, ca. 1880s, excellent condition, 9" h. (ILLUS.) **100**

Magic lantern, "Jung Amerika," upright rectangular wooden case w/domed top & tapering cylindrical chimney w/flared top, on small peg feet, excellent condition w/original burner & internal glass chimney, the round metal medallion on the side lifting up to permit adjustments to the burner wick, wooden case lifting off the base, Germany, probably made specifically for the American market, ca. 1880s, 11" h. (ILLUS. right) **575**

Magic lantern, "Lampadophore," by Lapierre, bronze, original bronze lacquer, lens, lens cap, no burner due to its being designed to be mounted on household oil lamp, France, ca. 1893, 15" h. (ILLUS. right) **400**

"Jung Amerika" Magic Lantern

15" "Lampadophore" Magic Lantern

Nickel-plated "Lampadophore"

Magic lantern, "Lampadophore," by Lapierre, upright nickel-plated type w/flaring cylindrical pedestal, spherical body w/lens & tall cylindrical chimney, burner works, completely original, France, ca. 1890s, overall 18 1/2" h. (ILLUS.) **1,300**

"Lampascope Carré" Magic Lantern

Magic lantern, "Lampascope Carré," by Lapierre, retains some original lacquer, comes w/nine early h.p. panorama-style slides, rare, France, ca. 1880, missing illuminant, 2 1/4 x 10 1/5", 12" h. (ILLUS.)..... **400**

Magic lantern, "Lantern Carrée," by Lapierre, metal case w/a few minor rust spots, scarcer smaller variant, France, ca. 1880s, 10" h. (illuminant missing).. **300**

14" "Lampadophore" Magic Lantern

Magic lantern, "Lampadophore," possibly by Lapierre, bronze, original bronze lacquer, lens, lens cap, no burner due to its being designed to be mounted on household oil lamp, 14" h. (ILLUS.) **380**

Early French Magic Lantern

Magic lantern, "Lantern Carrée," by Lapierre, square tinplate shape on small cylindrical legs, the sides punched w/a large star design & small circles in the corners, low pierced gallery around the top centered by the wide cylindrical chimney w/a fluted pyramidal cap w/ring handle, fine aged patina, excellent condition, burner missing, France, ca. 1845, 11" h. (ILLUS.)..... **450**

"Lanterne Carée" Magic Lantern

Magic lantern, "Lanterne Carée," by Lapierre, w/original burner, reflector & lens cap, France, ca. 1880, 11 1/2" h. (ILLUS.)..... **375**

LaPierre Lanterne "Medallion"

Magic lantern, "Lanterne Medallion," by Lapierre, original lacquer, rather pitted, w/original oil illuminant, scarce, France, ca. 1880, 12 1/2" h. (ILLUS.) **150**

Magic lantern, "Lanterne Medallion," by Lapierre, upright rectangular metal case w/large cylindrical chimney w/cap, origi-

nal colorful lacquer w/some minor pitting, France, ca. 1880, 10" h. (oil burner missing) **545**

Lapierre "Medallion" Magic Lantern

Magic lantern "Lanterne Medallion," by Lapierre, upright rectangular tinplate frame w/fluted panel sides, tall cylindrical chimney w/cap, some pitting on the original lacquer surface, w/original burner, reflector, lens caps & one slide, France, late 19th c., overall 14 1/2" h. (ILLUS.) **475**

Magic lantern, marked "The Empire," black metal upright rectangular body on tab feet, cylindrical angled top chimney, complete w/original burner & internal glass chimney, probably English or American, ca. 1880-90, 10 1/2" h................. **275**

"The Joung Amerikan" Magic Lantern

Magic lantern, marked "The Joung Ameri-kan," domed rectangular metal form w/cylindrical chimney at the top, complete w/burner & internal glass chimney, Germany, ca. 1890s (ILLUS.) **500**

Plank German Miniature Magic Lantern

Magic lantern, miniature, by Ernst Plank, red lacquer metal w/grey chimney, spherical body raised on stepped round base, w/original box & five slides, some wear spots on body, Germany, ca. 1895, 7" h. (ILLUS.) **350**

Primitive German Magic Lantern

Magic lantern, primitive, tin, comes w/what appears to be original oil burner, Germany, ca. 1860s, replacement cap on chimney, 9" h. (ILLUS.) **550**

Ernst Plank "Prophet" Magic Lantern

Magic lantern, "Prophet," by Ernst Plank, grey metal upright body on a flat rectangular base, very tall curved chimney, brassbound lens w/rack & pinion focusing, base painted to resemble wood, comes in original wooden box w/eight strip slides, each w/four circular images presumably originally sold w/the lantern, few minor rust spots, illuminant missing, Germany, ca. 1900, 18" h. (ILLUS.) **550**

Magic lantern, rectangular upright metal case w/long cylindrical lens housing w/bracket supports, w/original limelight illuminant, metal slide carrier w/some rust, body w/some rust, one of the elements of the condenser cracked, unknown maker, early 20th c. (ILLUS. top of next page) **110**

McAllister's New York Model Lantern

Magic lantern, "New York Model Magic Lantern," by T.H. McAllister, nickel-plated metal w/bellows in excellent condition, w/original oil illuminant, patent dated April 6, 1886 & November 22, 1887, one nickel-plated trade label slight damaged, chimney missing (ILLUS.) **200**

Magic Lantern by Unknown Maker

Steward Magic Lantern Projector

Magic lantern projector, by J.H. Steward, London, mahogany & brass, comes w/illuminant marked "Patent no. 1957, 3 wick Refulgent Lamp for Magic Lanterns," internal condensers present, w/telescoping chimney, in original wooden box w/lock & key, some missing black paint on lantern, ca. 1880s, 6 1/2 x 18", 10 1/2" h. without chimney (ILLUS.) **1,000**

Small Magic Lantern-Cinematograph

Magic lantern - Cinematograph combination, upright metal case w/high curved metal chimney, smaller toy version, original oil burner & internal glass chimney, minor chips to black paint, probably German, ca. 1900 (ILLUS.) **40**

Aphengascope by Jean Schoenner

Magic lantern-opaque projector combination, "Aphengascope," by Jean Schoenner, painted tinplate, upright rectangular case in bright red original paint w/twin black chimneys & an attractive cameo decal of a young lady on the back end, lacks illuminants, a few minor signs of wear, overall very good condition, Germany, ca. 1895, 8 1/2 x 12", 22" h. plus chimneys (ILLUS.) **400**

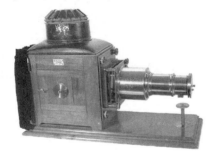

English Magic Lantern/Slide Projector

Magic lantern/slide projector, mahogany & brass, w/original gas jet illuminant, for projecting standard 4 x 7" mechanical & static slides as well as 3 1/4" sq. & 3 1/4 x 4" size using appropriate slide carriers, focal length can be reduced by unscrewing one of the brass lens barrels, marked "Newton & Co., Opticians To The Queen, 3, Fleet St., London," England, ca. 1905, 10 x 25" at base, 18 1/2" h. w/chimney (ILLUS.) **1,400**

Electric Magic Lantern/Slide Projector

Magic lantern/slide projector, mahogany & brass w/original lacquer, for projecting standard 4 x 7" mechanical & static slides as well as 3 1/4" sq. & 3 1/4 x 4" images by using appropriate slide carriers, unscrewing one of the brass lens barrels allows the lantern to be used in smaller spaces, w/original electric illuminant, marked "Newton & Co., Opticians To The Queen, 3, Fleet St., London," England, ca. 1895, 10 x 23", 22" h. (ILLUS.)............................. **1,400**

Magic lanterns, walnut & brass w/black-painted metal lamp houses, each w/a brass barreled "Darlot" lens w/rack & pinion focusing & brass lens cap, each professionally electrified & including a "Deon 4803" controller for fade & dissolve effects, wiring nearly new, excellent condition, late 19th c., each 20" l., 16" h., pr. **700**

"Magic Mirrorscope," brass barreled-form similar to a kaleidoscope except it does not revolve, a plano-convex lens in combination w/three internal mirrors gives a multi-image effect to whatever is being viewed, minor chip on plano-convex lens, overall excellent condition, probably 1920s, 8" l. (ILLUS. bottom of page)............ **175**

Brass "Magic Mirrorscope"

Tony Sarg "Magic Movie Book"

"Magic Movie Book," by Tony Sarg, five of the pages w/revolving wheels that show different illustrations, a pair of moveable Anaglyphic "glasses" included in a front pocket, when the glasses are moved alternating red & blue filters give the illustrations an animated movement, unusual example, published in 1943, slight soiling but overall very good condition (ILLUS.)...... **160**

Marcy's Sciopticon Magic Lantern

Marcy's "Sciopticon" magic lantern, brass w/original lacquer, original Darlot lens & Marcy two-wick burner w/patent dates of 1868 & 1869, internal shutter & filters present & working, in original box w/descriptive label on interior of lid, ca. 1870, missing small wire clip that holds slide in place, 18" l., 19" h. (ILLUS.) **440**

Marcy's "Sciopticon" Lantern Slide Projector

Marcy's "Sciopticon" magic lantern, w/brass-barreled "Darlot" lens, converted to electricity some years ago, ca. 1870s (ILLUS.)... **150**

Megalethoscope from Italy

Megalethoscope, by Carlo Ponti, comes w/12 photographic Italian views, scarce, Italy, ca. 1860s, original mirrors somewhat cloudy & missing some silver, 20 x 36", 24" h. (ILLUS.) **5,750**

Megalethoscope, by Carlo Ponti, Venice, Italy, very fine example w/the case in walnut w/carved panels featuring various allegorical figures representing scientific achievements, one panel shows a figure w/a camera, all lenses & internal holders & masks present, overall excellent condition, on a high rectangular storage cabinet base w/paneled doors & sides, includes 15 views showing various day/night effects, ca. 1870s, case, probably not original to the viewer, measures 21 x 27 1/2", 27 1/2" h., viewer 20 x 36", 24" h. (ILLUS.) **10,500**

"Midgette Movies" flick-book viewer, metal case w/small crank handle, designed to hold four flick books but only three are present, w/worn original box, ca. 1950s (ILLUS.) **180**

Mono Viewer for Autochromes

Mono Autochrome viewer, by the London Stereoscopic Co., designed to hold 24 mono quarter-plate autochromes, rack & pinion focusing mechanism, cabinet opens to facilitate easy loading of new images, comes w/23 autochromes, rare, ca. 1910, 4 1/4 x 13" at base, 15 1/4" h. (ILLUS.) **4,000**

"Midgette Movies" Flick-Book Viewer & Box

Floor-standing Coin-op "Mutoscope"

Mutoscope, tin plate & cast iron w/wooden stand & marquee, floor-standing coin-op model, w/winding mechanism, comes w/one complete reel of exotic dancer, 1920s, repainted, new locks & keys, 17" h. (ILLUS.) **3,000**

"World Syndicate" Movie Machine

Mutoscope, "World Syndicate - Newspaper Movie Machine," upright cylindrical tin-plate case w/original decoration & small crank handle, displays newspaper cutouts, United States, ca. 1919, excellent condition, 2 x 5", 5" h. (ILLUS.) **700**

"Ombres Chinoises" viewer, in box containing theater marquee, seven silhouette shadow cutouts & two wire holders, very colorful, 7 1/2 x 10" (ILLUS. top of next page) **200**

Opaque projector, "Dux Episcope," Bakelite case w/working opaque projector w/a great 1950s look, w/instructions in original box, Germany, ca. 1950s (ILLUS. middle of next page) **55**

"Foto-Scope" Opaque Projector

Opaque projector, "Foto-Scope," by Stratton Mfg. Co., New York, New York, rectangular metal box-form on short legs, minor dings & scratches, ca. 1920s, 6 x 9", 7" h. (ILLUS.) **60**

"Ombres Chinoises" Viewer

1950s "Dux Episcope" Projector

Unique Panorama-style Photograph Viewer

Panorama-style photograph viewer, reputed to be made by a Mr. Elan Mitchell of pieces of wood, hand-shaped to accommodate the two interior spools, each spool turned w/removable hand crank attached to brass turning pin in center of spool, advancing each photograph into position for the 4" d. magnifying lens, comes w/about 50 mounted photographs on continuous fabric reel, unique, America, late 19th c., 13 x 18" (ILLUS.) **1,800**

Adams & Co. "Pantoscope" Viewer

"Pantoscope," by Adams & Co, binocular table-top model, mahogany case raised on fancy scroll-cut trestle base, resembles a stereoscope but designed to view magic lantern slides, excellent condition, England, ca. 1892, 10" h. (ILLUS.) **1,300**

Early Peep Show Toy of the Thames Tunnel

Peep show toy, folded paper, illustrates the Thames Tunnel, extends out to form a long deep panorama viewed through a hole at the end, colors inside are very fresh & clean, exterior w/some soil & some corner reinforcement on the lid, this example w/a lower double aperture showing the exterior of the tunnel while the single aperture at the top shows the surface of the Thames, ca. 1850, above average condition, ends measure 6 1/2 x 7 3/4", opens to 24" l. (ILLUS. top of page) **900**

Praxinoscope, "Kinematofor," by Ernst Plank, 6" d. drum, comes w/three multi-colored animated strips, in original box w/tape reinforcement, Germany, ca. 1895, 6 1/2" h. (ILLUS.) **800-1,200**

Praxinoscope optical toy, by Emil Reynaud, metal wheel raised on a low turned wood base, candleholder at top center w/reproduction paneled shade w/advertising, w/four animated strips, some minor wear but overall excellent condition, France, ca. 1877 .... **1,500**

"Kinematofor" Praxinoscope

"Magic Mirror" Turntable Viewer

Red Raven "Magic Mirror" turntable viewer, animation record & mirror are placed on turntable & animation on record is viewed through angled mirror, comes w/two double-sided records w/mirror, America, ca. 1956 (ILLUS.)........... **225**

Reflecting Viewer Optical Toy

Reflecting viewer optical toy, w/approximately 4" d. concave mirror in which views of high quality reverse-printed cards are reflected, giving a pseudo stereoscopic effect, comes w/three complete sets of eight cards based on magic lantern slides of the "Primus" series (ILLUS.) **80**

Reversing, Reflecting Mirror Viewer

Reversing, reflecting mirror viewer, the 4 1/2" d. mirror viewer both magnifying & giving pseudo stereoscopic effect, w/two sets of eight 3 1/2 x 5 1/2" magic lantern cards each, printed in reverse to show correctly in mirror, can also be used in mirror-style opaque projectors, each set w/its own "Lantern Lecture" reading material (ILLUS.) **120**

"Rotophoto" Movie Viewer

"Rotophoto" movie viewer, based on the flicker book principal, w/crank winding movement, red paint, comes w/some real photographs of Western action scenes, Germany, ca. 1920s (ILLUS.) **750**

Eighteenth Century Scioptric Ball

Scioptric ball, the original ball & lens mounted in a disc-style replicated turned wood framed, lens w/focal length of about five feet, used mainly for making Panorama drawings, 18th c. (ILLUS.) **1,700**

1977 Souvenir Peep Show Toy

Souvenir peep show toy, lithographed expandable paper, ten-section type, a souvenir from the 1977 Silver Jubilee of Queen Elizabeth II, excellent condition in original slip case box (ILLUS.) **35**

Souvenir Photograph Viewer of 1937 World's Fair

Souvenir photograph viewer, Art Deco style, "Souvenir de L'Exposition Internationale - Paris - 1937" on front, contains 18 real photo images of buildings at the Fair on continuous roll, France, 2 1/2 x 4" (ILLUS.).. **160**

Advertising Thaumatrope

Thaumatrope, paper advertising-type w/images of a boy & spool of thread promoting Clark's Spool Cotton, good color, ca. 1890s, 2 1/4 x 3 1/2" (ILLUS.)................ **130**

"The Myriopticon, A Historical Panorama (of the) Rebellion," by Milton Bradley, revolving panorama toy showing scenes of the Civil War, lecture script present, early replacement handle, operates well, excellent condition in original box w/some corner wear, ca. 1870, box 5 x 8" **850**

"The Myriopticon" Revolving Panorama

"The Myriopticon" revolving panorama, by Milton Bradley, "A Historical Panorama (of the) Rebellion," showing scenes from the Civil War, in original box w/lecture script, tickets & a broadside, retailer's label on box reads "Presented with the Compliments of E.S. Fay, Boots & Shoes, Holyoke, Mass.," scarce, ca. 1870, diorama roll w/repaired tear, lecture script somewhat stained, broadside torn at folds, handle not original, 5 x 8" (ILLUS.).. **950**

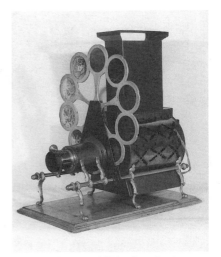

New Improved Sciopticon Lantern

"The New Improved Sciopticon Lantern - with Revolving Disc," by The Pettibone Mfg. Co., Cincinnati, Ohio, plate metal, w/original factory electrification, carefully replicated chimney added, comes w/two revolving discs each w/10 colored round images as well as a carrier for standard sized glass slides, all in original storage-shipping trunk w/old labels, ca. 1890s, excellent condition, 11 x 20", 13" h. without chimney (ILLUS.) . **2,500**

"The Novitascope" Optical Toy

"The Novitascope" optical toy, usually referred to as a Phenakistascope, w/five double-sided 3 3/4" d. animation discs, one 6" d. slotted viewing disc & wire rod, in original box, The Novitas Sales Co., Waltham, Massachusetts, ca. 1910 (ILLUS.) **1,100**

"The Uniscope" Viewing Box

"The Uniscope," lithographed tin peep/view box for postcards or photographs w/magnifying lens in the front, Patent No. 11139, England, ca. 1900, worn blue color (ILLUS.) **90**

"The Uniscope" Viewing Box from England

"The Uniscope," tin plate, peep/view box for postcards or photographs, Patent no. 11139, magnifying lens in front, blue w/gold highlights, England (ILLUS.) **80**

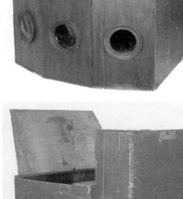

Three-person Showman's Peepshow

Three-person Showman's Peepshow, the rear box w/slots for 12 perspective views that are raised & lowered by the Showman by a simple string pulley system, comes w/12 views, extremely rare, probably France, ca. 1820, nine views have significant damage, viewing box missing rear reflecting panel, several small pieces of trim missing, 22 x 27", 21" h. at rear (ILLUS.).. **7,500**

Toy telescope, cardboard, by Marks Bros. Co., two-drawer, w/colorful decal, ca. 1930s, missing objective lens, 15" l. closed, 31" l. extended (ILLUS. bottom of page) **30**

Marks Bros. Toy Telescope

Early "Vioptican" Electric Slide Projector

"Vioptican" Model 3 slide projector, by the Victor Animatograph Co., horizontal tapering cylindrical shape, w/original electrical arc illuminant & a wooden slide carrier for 2" slides, some rust marks on lamp house, patented May 27, 1913, overall very good condition, 14" l. (ILLUS.)................ **110**

Zillograph Shadow Theater

Zoetrope, "Cinematographe - Enfantin," 10" d. cardboard drum covered in blue paper matches darker blue base, comes w/two double-sided multicolored strips, rare, France, ca. 1880, 11" h. **1,452**

Rare "Whirligig of Life" Praxinoscope

"Whirligig of Life" Praxinoscope, by McLoughlin Bros., New York, New York, scope all-original but a couple of the mirrors show slight desilvering, w/six original animated strips, overall excellent condition, rare, ca. 1880s (ILLUS.) **800-1,200**

"Zillograph" shadow theater, "Faces with Changing Expressions," in original box w/eight moveable shadow/silhouette images on thick cardboard & a projection screen, very unusual, ca. 1890-1900, 10 x 10" box (ILLUS. following) **375**

"Cinematographe - Enfantin" Zoetrope

Zoetrope, "Cinematographe - Enfantin," in blue embossed cardboard w/matching blue base, comes w/six original animated strips & lid, rare, France, ca. 1890s, 9 1/2" d. drum, 11" h. (ILLUS. previous page) **1,300**

Early English Zoetrope Toy

Zoetrope, composed of 11" d. metal drum on turned mahogany pedestal base, apparently all-original w/three animated disks, 10 colored & 16 black & white animated strips, minor wear to finish of drum, a couple of the black & white strips partially colored, all strips reinforced on the back w/1872 newspaper, some strips w/small tears, England, ca. 1872, the group (ILLUS.).. **1,200**

London Stereoscopic Company Zoetrope

Zoetrope, London Stereoscopic Company, ca. 1870s (ILLUS.)......... **1,000-1,500**

Early Miniature Zoetrope

Zoetrope, miniature, black cardboard drum on a turned wood base, comes w/six double-sided animated strips, very good condition, ca. 1890s, drum 5" d., overall 7" h. (ILLUS.) **360**

"Spin-e-ma" Zoetrope on New Base

Zoetrope, "Spin-e-ma," black metal drum came w/handle to spin on, includes handle & six multicolored animation strips, shown w/specially-made turned base, drum 7" d., England, ca. 1920s (ILLUS.) **200**

Tin Zoetrope

Zoetrope, tin drum probably originally held candy or some other confection, the lid doubling as base on which the 5" d. 4 1/2" h. drum spins, comes w/three animated strips, England or France, ca. 1890 (ILLUS.)... **303**

Zoetrope, "Witt's 4-in-1 Moviescope," w/original 20 animated strips, all in original box, scarce in this exceptionally fine condition, America, ca. 1910, original box w/some tape reinforcements (ILLUS. bottom of page)... **585**

Zoetrope, "Witt's 4-in-1 Moviescope," designed to be handheld or placed on a gramophone turntable or a spindle under the box lid, 7" d. drum, comes w/10 double-sided animation strips & the original box, box & lid repaired w/colorful label intact, America, ca. 1910 .... **400**

English "Zograscope"

"Zograscope," comes w/one hand-colored engraving of the Port of Calais, England, late 18th - early 19th c., 29" h. fully extended (ILLUS.)... **650**

"Whitt's 4-in-1 Moviescope" Zoetrope

CHAPTER 4
Magic Lantern & Optical Toy Accessories

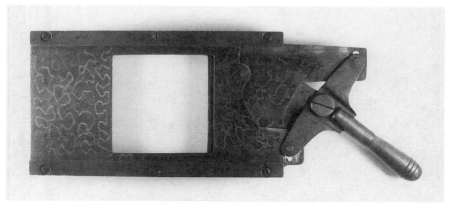

Rare Dissolving Shutter for Lantern Slide Projector

Bi-Unial Projector

Biunial slide projector, w/Bausch & Lomb lenses, America, early 20th c., small door missing from rear of top lamp housing, needs rewiring, 22 1/2" h. (ILLUS.) $325

Dissolving shutter for lantern slide projector, flat rectangular form, shutter opens & closes by means of a lever on the side, designed to fit over a lens barrel about 2" to 3" d., excellent condition, ca. 1870s (ILLUS. top of page) 200

Kinora Reel #270 - shows a sports day event with people in a sack race, excellent condition in original box 200

Kinora Reel #526 - "Launching of the Newquay Lifeboat," shows a lifeboat launching, excellent condition in original box w/torn lid 110

Kinora Reel #542 - shows ice skating & children's ice hockey, excellent condition in original box 110

Kinora Reel #63 - "German Gunboat Firing Torpedoes," shows a two-stack torpedo boat under full steam, excellent condition in original box 80

Kinora Reel #64 - "The Stable on Fire," shows horses running from a burning barn, excellent condition in original box 120

Magic lantern illuminant, three-wick kerosene-style, rectangular metal design, overall good condition, ca. 1870s (some rust) 55

Peepshow perspective views, group of twenty, nineteen views w/holes or cutouts for back lights in a peep box or perspective viewer, subjects mostly European architecture, most views hand-colored, all w/titles in Dutch, various conditions from fair to very good, in apparently original oak storage box, Europe, ca. 1800, the set 2,750

Perspective view for a Peepshow, a view titled in French show the Strand in London, England, w/holes or cutouts for backlighting in a peep box or perspective viewer, ca. 1800, slight soil, trimmed slightly at bottom, overall very good condition, 11 1/4 x 18" (ILLUS. top of next page) 130

Perspective view for a Peepshow, an interior view of a theatre in Naples, Italy, titled in French, w/holes or cutouts for backlighting in a peep box or perspective viewer, overall very good condition, early & rare, ca. 1800, 10 1/4 x 18" (ILLUS. bottom of next page) 130

Early Peepshow Perspective View of London

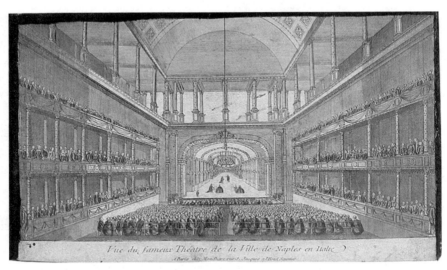

Early Perspective View of a Theatre in Naples

Early Peepshow Perspective View of a Chinese Temple

Perspective view for a Peepshow, view titled in French showing a Chinese temple interior, w/holes & cutouts for backlighting, some slight soil & trimmed slightly at the bottom, overall very good condition, ca. 1800, 11 1/2 x 18" (ILLUS. top of page) **130**

Magic Lantern Microscope Attachment

Projecting microscope attachment & slides, for a magic lantern, a brass barreled lens & right angle mirror attachment together w/six wooden slides all in the original fitted box, all brass w/original lacquer, interior lock on box missing, otherwise excellent condition, ca. 1870s, the set (ILLUS.) **750**

"Eclipse Patent Arc Lamp, No. 344,"

Ross "Eclipse Patent Arc Lamp, No. 344," complex metal apparatus, well-made carbon arc illuminant for a projection device, several precise adjustment movements, excellent condition, Thomas Ross & Co., England, late 19th c. (ILLUS.) **125**

Transposing View of L'Hotel de Ville, Paris, France

Transposing View of La Sainte Chapelle, Paris, France

Transposing View of Notre Dame Cathedral in Paris

Magic Lantern Slide Carrier

Slide carrier, wood, for standard English 3 1/4" sq. slides (ILLUS.) 35

Slide carrier, wood, made for standard English lantern slides by Archer, 3 1/4" sq. (small chip to bottom not affecting the operation) 40

Transposing view of L'Hotel de Ville, Paris, die-cut day/night scene, sold by the Paris department store Le Bon Marche, great Art Nouveau border design, very colorful & good day/night effect, excellent condition, ca. 1890, 4 1/2 x 6 1/2" (ILLUS. top of previous page) 65

Transposing view of La Sainte Chapelle, Paris, die-cut day/night scene, sold by the Paris department store Le Bon Marche, very colorful & good day/night effect, excellent condition, ca. 1890, 4 1/2 x 6 1/2" (ILLUS. bottom of previous page) 55

Transposing view of Notre Dame Cathedral, Paris, die-cut day/night scene, sold by the Paris department store Le Bon Marche, very colorful & good day-night effect, excellent condition, ca. 1890, 4 1/2 x 6 1/2" (ILLUS. top of page) 55

CHAPTER 5
Magic Lantern Slides

"A Christmas Carol"
Magic Lantern Slide Set

"A Christmas Carol" set, h.p. wood mounted slides illustrating Dickens' classic tale, w/photocopy of original lantern reading, rare, set of 12 (ILLUS. left and page 99).. **$450**

Acrobatic monkey silhouette slide, mounted in a flat wooden frame w/end crank handle, the pulley sometimes slips but is easily corrected, scarce, 19th c. (ILLUS. page 100)...................................... **225**

Alice in Wonderland series, complete set of 24 slides in three boxes, no reading, boxes rather worn, slides excellent, England, ca. 1900, the set.......................... **278**

Allegorical patriotic design, wood-framed, titled "Columbia - Home of the Free," colorful scene showing Columbia seated on a throne w/Washington & Lincoln flanking her, all surrounded by a crowd, excellent condition, 4 x 7"................... **85**

Artist sitting on river bank, single slip mechanical-type, slips to reveal a soldier behind him putting a gun to his head, excellent condition.. **250**

Astronomical view, single rackwork mechanical-type, paper label reads "No. 9 - The Diagram shows the various Eclipses of the Sun, with the Transit of Venus," some skillful restoration to the paint but overall excellent condition.......................... **170**

Aurora Borealis, static h.p. type, Arctic scene, shows the Aurora Borealis (Northern Lights), excellent condition...................... **25**

Australian views, complete box of eight from "Our Colonies" series, England, ca. 1900, no reading, excellent condition, the set **20**

Cat on Barrel Magic Lantern Slide

Barrel, single slip mechanical-type, wood mounted, chromolithograph of barrel

"A Christmas Carol" Magic Lantern Slide Set

Acrobatic Monkey Silhouette Slide

marked "Old Tom" slips to reveal cat on top of the barrel, 4 x 7" (ILLUS. page 98) **40**

Battle scene, wood-framed, untitled but appears to be the Battle of New Orleans, excellent condition, 4 x 7" **31**

Beehive with bees, double rackwork mechanical-type, shows bees swarming all around hive, good effect of movement, very colorful, excellent condition **355**

Begging man, combination single slip h.p. pivoted-lever mechanical-type, shows a man begging, the pivot moves the man's hand up & down, the slide brings a young girl to drop some change into his hat, very good condition (slight paint loss to figure, some skillful restoration) **170**

Black Lecturer Magic Lantern Slide

Black lecturer, single lever mechanical-type, wood mounted, h.p. image of black man at lecture table facing black audience, lever moves lecturer's body, 4 x 7" (ILLUS.) **85**

"Bonne Nuit" Magic Lantern Slide

"Bonne Nuit" (Good Night) single slip mechanical-type, wood mounted, h.p. image of yawning woman in night gown &

cap, slips to show words "Bonne Nuit," 4 x 7" (ILLUS.).. **40**

British gunboat, single lever h.p. mechanical-type, shows a British gunboat under full sail on a moonlit night, lever rocks the ship back & forth, beautiful scene, excellent condition.. **325**

Carnation bud, double slip mechanical-type, slips to reveal the carnation in full bloom, beautiful color, excellent condition **50**

Chicken egg, single slip mechanical-type, slips to reveal a newborn chick emerging from the egg, excellent condition **100**

"Christmas Eve in Camp," static hand-painted type, Civil War era, titled "535. Christmas Eve in Camp," excellent condition **65**

Circus clown, double slip h.p. mechanical-type, shows a circus clown doing an acrobatic jump over a horse, double slip shows the clown in three different positions, great effect, excellent condition.......... **275**

Circus clown, single slip mechanical-type, slips to show the clown has broken into pieces, excellent condition **35**

Circus Juggler Magic Lantern Slide

Circus performer, single slip mechanical-type, wood mounted, chromolithograph of circus performer juggling ball w/his feet, slips to give illusion of movement, 4 x 7" (ILLUS.).. **70**

Civil War related, wood-framed, a pair of slides illustrating "The Brave Drummer Boy and his Father," one shows a Civil War drummer boy & his father leading the charge, the second shows them mortally wounded on the battlefield w/a dream illustration of them being welcomed to heaven, rich & colorful, each 4 x 7", the pair **100**

Civil War related, wood-framed glass, titled "Home from the War," shows a wounded soldier inside his home being comforted by his wife & daughter, colorfully painted, excellent condition, 4 x 7" **33**

Civil War related, wood-framed, titled "Altoona Pass or Hold the Fort," shows a raging battle w/a Confederate battle flag in the foreground, colorfully painted, excellent condition, 4 x 7" **46**

Civil War related, wood-framed, titled "Grand Army (of the) Republic," shows a Union soldier on guard duty in the middle of a rainstorm, colorfully painted, excellent condition, 4 x 7" **40**

Civil War related, wood-framed, titled "The Fight for the Flag," shows a mounted cavalry man on a white horse holding the U.S. flag while stabbing an enemy soldier w/his saber, colorfully painted, excellent condition, 4 x 7" **44**

Clown in front of large bottle, single slip mechanical-type, slips to reveal a Harlequin figure jumping out of the bottle, excellent condition **150**

"Cook & the Flying Goose"
Magic Lantern Slide

"Cook & the Flying Goose," single slip mechanical-type, wood mounted, h.p. image of woman, slips to reveal her nose extended w/bump on the end, 4 x 7" (ILLUS.) **50**

"Cour de David in Jerusalem," single slip h.p. panoramic mechanical-type, shows a moonlit desert castle, several people slide across on horseback, camel & foot in silhouette, a hard-to-read paper label in French reads "Cour de David in Jerusalem," beautiful scene, excellent condition, 4 x 11".. **275**

Crescent moon, single slip mechanical-type, lithographic view, slips to become an old woman w/the printed legend "Luna Caustic," excellent condition **41**

"Cutting Corns," single slip h.p. mechanical-type, titled "Cutting Corns," shows a man with an axe cutting his corns, excellent condition **35**

Dancing clown, single slip h.p. mechanical-type, shows a dancing clown, excellent illusion of movement, excellent condition.......... **40**

Diagram of the Earth, astronomical single rackwork mechanical-type, paper label reads "No. 5, A Diagram to prove the Earth's Rotundity," excellent condition **150**

Eclipses of the Moon, astronomical rackwork mechanical-type, shows full & partial eclipses of the moon, excellent condition **150**

Egyptian scenes, dissolving-type, pair of tinted photographic slides titled "Pyramids and Sphinx, Egypt (Day) & (Night)," excellent condition, pr. **148**

Elephant on its back, single slip mechanical-type, slip reveals it juggling a baby elephant, excellent condition **77**

English policeman w/flashlight, single lever mechanical-type, lever moves to show a beam of light, overall excellent condition... **80**

Father Time with a cannon, single slip mechanical-type, slip shows the cannon firing food & drink, New Year's theme, excellent condition **117**

Fighting Men Magic Lantern Slide

"Clown's Transformation" Magic Lantern Slide

"Clown's Transformation," single slip mechanical-type, wood mounted, h.p. image of clown's head slips to transform his head into that of an ass, 4 x 7" (ILLUS.) **45**

Fighting men, single slip mechanical-type, wood mounted, h.p. image of man falling slips to reveal man punching him on the nose, 4 x 7" (ILLUS.) **40**

Fisherman head & shoulder view, single slip mechanical-type, slip shows only his eyes moving, effective & colorful, excellent condition **40**

Girl on Swing Magic Lantern Slide

Girl on swing, single slip mechanical-type, wood mounted, h.p. image of girl on swing, slip moves the girl to & fro in illusion of movement, 4 x 7" (ILLUS.) **80**

"Good Night" single slip h.p. mechanical-type, shows a floral wreath, slips to reveal "Good Night," excellent condition **40**

Pixie Riding Goose Magic Lantern Slide

Goose, single slip mechanical-type, wood mounted, h.p. image of running goose w/wings outstretched slips to reveal pixie-like figure riding goose, 4 x 7" (ILLUS.) **50**

Harbor scene, unusual black & white photographic panoramic lantern slide of harbor scene, probably Mediterranean France, 3 1/2 x 9 1/2" (ILLUS. bottom of page) **35**

Dancing Highlander Magic Lantern Slide

Highlander, single slip mechanical-type, wood mounted, h.p. image of kilted Highlander dancing a reel or jig slips to show movement, 4 x 7" (ILLUS.)............................. **45**

Kaleidoscope-type, double rackwork Chromatrope mechanical-type, great

Panoramic Slide of Harbor Scene

multicolored effect, excellent condition, slightly oversized, 4 2/3 x 8 1/2".................. **200**

Kaleidoscope-type, double rackwork Chromatrope mechanical-type, multicolored star pattern kaleidoscopic effect, excellent condition **317**

Kaleidoscope-type, double rackwork Chromatrope mechanical-type, unusual off-center multicolored kaleidoscopic effect, excellent condition............................... **532**

Kaleidoscopic Magic Lantern Slide

Kaleidoscope-type, double rackwork Chromatrope mechanical-type, wood mounted, h.p. kaleidoscopic image, 4 x 7" (ILLUS.)... **275**

Kaleidoscope-type, early double pulley Chromatrope mechanical-type, multicolored effect, very good to excellent condition (ILLUS. bottom of page) **484**

"Last Moments of Maximillian," woodframed, single slide showing the Mexican emperor kneeling in prayer before his execution, part of a series, excellent condition, 4 x 7" **10**

Man being shaved by a barber, single slip mechanical-type, slip moves the barber's arm back & forth (slip glass chipped & w/a small crack but does not affect projection of image)... **72**

Man carrying a pig, single slip mechanical-type, slips to reveal the pig jumping to the ground, excellent condition **35**

Man Carving Turkey Magic Lantern Slide

Man carving turkey, single slip mechanical-type, wood mounted, h.p. image of man carving turkey at table, slips to reveal him carving turkey from floor, 4 x 7" (ILLUS.)... **70**

Man & crocodile, single slip h.p. mechanical-type, shows a man about to dive in a river, slips to reveal he has jumped into a crocodile's mouth, excellent condition **40**

Man Eating Turtle Soup Magic Lantern Slide

Man eating turtle soup, single slip mechanical-type, wood mounted, h.p. image of man eating soup, slips to reveal

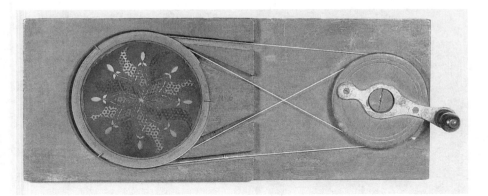

Kaleidoscopic Double Pulley Chromatrope Mechanical Slide

that the turtle has jumped out & is biting man's nose, 4 x 7" (ILLUS.) **70**

Man going to bed, single slip h.p. mechanical-type, shows a man about to get into bed, slips to reveal hands about to grab him, excellent condition.................................. **90**

Man holding frying pan over fire, single slip mechanical-type, black-painted wood w/brass pull, slips to reveal the man's head in the frying pan, early, 4 1/2 x 9 1/2" **300**

Man & parrot, double slip h.p. mechanical-type, shows a man sitting in a chair reading, a parrot on the back of the chair, slips to reveal the parrot has pulled off the man's wig, excellent condition...................... **45**

Man reading newspaper by candlelight, single slip mechanical-type, slip reveals the candle has set his hair on fire, excellent condition **66**

Man riding donkey, single slip mechanical-type, wood mounted, h.p. image of man on donkey, slips to reveal donkey trying to toss man off as man beats donkey, 4 x 7"........ **35**

Man sitting on seashore looking through a telescope, single slip mechanical-type, slip reveals a deep sea diver coming out of the water, excellent condition..................... **65**

Man walking with basket & umbrella, single slip mechanical-type, slip reveals the umbrella balanced on his nose **90**

Man's face, single lever mechanical-type, nose, mouth & eyebrows move, giving an unusual morphing effect, excellent condition **257**

Military figures, single slip mechanical-type, two figures, possibly Russian, slips to reveal them having a sword fight, good illusion of movement, excellent condition....... **35**

Monkey & Dog Magic Lantern Slide

Monkey & dog, single lever mechanical-type, wood mounted, h.p. image of dressed monkey appearing to fan flames of a fire w/dog, 4 x 7" (ILLUS.) **40**

Monkey & Old Woman Slide

Monkey & old woman, single slip mechanical-type, wood mounted, h.p. image of old woman sitting in chair, a monkey perched on the back, slips to reveal the monkey pulling off the woman's cap, 4 x 7" (ILLUS.).. **45**

Moon & Earth, astronomical rackwork mechanical slide, shows the moon revolving around the Earth w/varying phases of the moon, excellent condition **154**

New Zealand views, complete boxed set of eight from "Our Colonies" series, no reading, England, ca. 1900, excellent condition, the set.. **50**

Panoramic style, rare early single slipping slide, titled "The Dry Arch Virginia Waters, Windsor - King in the Pony Phaeton," fabulous scene of King William IV & his entourage going past the arch, rich & colorful, excellent condition, ca. 1830s, 4 1/2 x 19".. **665**

Panoramic style, rare early slipping Phantasmagoria slide titled "Monsters," shows five different monsters w/eyes that move, very colorful, excellent condition, 4 1/2 x 19" **585**

Peter Pan series, complete set of 24 slides in three boxes, no reading, boxes rather worn but slides excellent, England, ca. 1900, the set **71**

Pineapple, single slip mechanical-type, slips to reveal the pineapple turned into a man's head, a few scratches on the black background but otherwise excellent condition **80**

Punch-style clown figure, single slip mechanical-type, slip elongates his nose & a small dog perched on the end, excellent condition.. **75**

Roller blind snow effect, flat wooden frame w/small end handles, used in combination w/any winter scene or Christmas slide to give the effect of snowfall, excellent condition, 19th c. (ILLUS. top of next page).. **325**

Ruins of abbey, single slip h.p. panoramic mechanical-type, shows a ruined church, several people on horseback & foot slide by in silhouette, hard-to-read paper label in French indicates this is a view of the Ruins of Cockburn Abbey (?), England, beautiful scene, excellent condition, 4 x 11".. **325**

Sailor bending over, single slip mechanical-type, slips to reveal a crocodile or sea monster biting him on the bottom, excellent condition... **30**

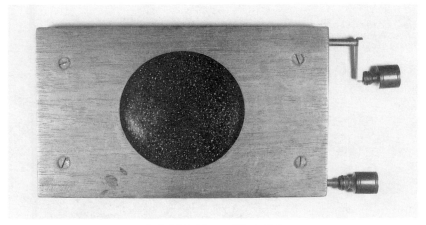

Roller Blind Snow Effect Slide

Sailor on Horseback Magic Lantern Slide

Sailor on horseback, single slip mechanical-type, wood mounted, h.p. image of sailor standing on horse dancing & waving flags, slip showing movement, 4 x 7" (ILLUS.)... **95**
Scottish views, group of 25 hand-tinted photographic slides of Scotland by G. Washington Wilson, very well done & finely tinted, excellent condition, also two other black & white slides of Scotland, England, late 19th c., the group **116**
Ship at sea scene, rare eccentric movement mechanical-type, titled "City of New York - Atlantic Liner," shows a combination sail & steam vessel under way under a moonlit sky, great sense of movement on the waves, rich & colorful, excellent condition **565**

Sailing Ship Magic Lantern Slide

Ship on ocean, single lever mechanical-type, wood mounted, h.p. image of sailing ship, the lever moving the ship in a pitching & tossing movement, 4 x 7" (ILLUS.)............. **160**
Slide set, boxed multiple rackwork mechanical slide set composed of six 3 1/2" sq. slides & six 3 1/2" d. matching round slides, each pair inserted in the special rackwork Chromatrope to form the following moving effect slides - "Rat Eater," "Windmill," "Witch," "Sleepy Gardener," "What the Sailor Saw in the Moon" & "Father Neptune," rare set (ILLUS. top of next page) **1,650**

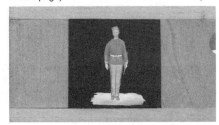

*Rare Boxed Set of
Multiple Rackwork
Mechanical Slides*

Magic Lantern Slide of Soldier

Soldier, single slip mechanical-type, wood mounted, h.p. image of soldier standing at attention slips to reveal him saluting, 4 x 7" (ILLUS. also on bottom of previous page) **40**

"Taking Off Boots" Magic Lantern Slide

"Taking Off Boots," single slip mechanical-type, wood mounted, h.p. image of boy pulling boots off seated man, slips to reveal boy has fallen over, 4 x 7" (ILLUS.)......... **40**

Temperance series, complete set of 50 slides titled "A Famous Orator - an Evening with John B. Gough," the title slide w/flags of Great Britain & the United States flanking a portrait of Gough, slides h.p. & colorful, all excellent condition except one w/small crack, in original wooden box, England, late 19th c., the set **199**

Temperance theme, wood-framed, titled "Three Members of the Temperance Society," colorfully painted scene of three horses drinking at a water trough, excellent condition, 4 x 7"....................................... **14**

"Ten Little Nigger Boys" series, complete set of eight slides, text of the nursery rhyme on each slide, excellent condition, England, ca. 1900, the set **162**

*"The Long & the Short of It"
Magic Lantern Slide*

"The Long & the Short of It," single slip mechanical-type, wood mounted, h.p. image of tall soldier slips to reveal him looking down at very short drummer, 4 x 7" (ILLUS.).. **45**

"The Sinking of the Maine," static h.p. type, Spanish American War era, titled "The Sinking of the Maine," excellent condition.. **15**

Two Boys Fighting Magic Lantern Slide

Two boys fighting, single slip mechanical-type, wood mounted, h.p. image of two boys w/fists raised, slips to reveal man either about to stop the fight or referee it, 4 x 7" (ILLUS.).. **40**

Two London Scene Lantern Slides

Views of London, England, group of eight 3 1/2" sq. black & white photographic views of London, excellent condition, ca. 1900, the group (ILLUS. of two).................. **180**

"What happens to naughty boys," single lever h.p. mechanical-type, shows a schoolmaster caning a boy, titled "What happens to naughty boys," good illusion of movement, excellent condition, slightly oversized, 4 1/2 x 7"..................................... **180**

"Wheel of Life" mechanical slide, composed of a glass revolving disc combined w/a shutter that revolves in the opposite direction, creating the illusion of a revolving six-pointed star similar in principal to a Phenakistascope, overall excellent condition, completely original, ca. 1869, 4 x 9" (ILLUS. bottom of page).................. **1,400**

"Whistling Boy," single slip h.p. mechanical-type, titled "Whistling Boy," shows a close-up view of a boy's face, only the eyes & mouth move, excellent condition........ **45**

Woman holding pudding over her head, single slip mechanical-type, slips to reveal a little boy crying because he can't reach the pudding, excellent condition........... **35**

Rare "Wheel of Life" Mechanical Slide

Woman puffing on pipe, single slip mechanical-type, slips to reveal head turned & blowing smoke in other direction **61**

Woman rocking baby, single lever h.p. mechanical-type, shows an African-American woman rocking a baby, excellent condition **65**

Woman taking pie out of cupboard, single slip mechanical-type, slips to reveal a little boy holding a slice of pie, excellent condition **42**

Woman with fan dancing, single slip h.p. mechanical-type, shows an African-American woman dancing with a fan in her hand, good illustration of movement, excellent condition **35**

Women talking, single slip mechanical-type, two well-dressed women, slips to review their heads have been replaced w/two bird heads, the pull skillfully repaired, otherwise excellent condition **30**

Young man skipping rope, pivoted lever mechanical-type, the fancily dressed man skipping, w/lever movement showing the rope ends held by two others, excellent condition **90**

CHAPTER 6
Stereoscopes & Viewers

"Achromatic" Stereoscope

R.J. Beck "Achromatic" Stereoscope

"Achromatic" stereoscope, by R.J. Beck, mahogany & brass, box holds viewer & views, England, patent date of 1859 (ILLUS.) **$1,100**

"Achromatic" stereoscope, by R.J. Beck, mahogany & brass, the box doubling as storage box for viewer or views, England, patent date 1859, mirror under reflecting lid w/significant silver loss doesn't affect operation (ILLUS. top of page) **2,000**

"Achromatic" Stereoscope

"Achromatic" stereoscope, mahogany & brass, by R.J. Beck, box doubles as storage box for viewer or views, w/additional reflector for use w/glass or tissue views, England, patent date 1859, considerable silver missing from original reflecting lid/mirror (ILLUS.) **1,028**

Advertising stereo viewer, miniature folding-type in tinplate decorated w/colorful

Art Deco designs, printed advertising for Suchard Chocolate & Cocoa, France, ca. 1930s, w/three mini views measuring 1 1/4 x 2 3/4", overall excellent condition..... **130**

Ca. 1859 Alexander Beckers Stereoscope

Beckers (Alexander) stereoscope, rosewood, tabletop model, pair of viewing lenses either side of cabinet, lens panel on one side slides down while ground glass diffusing screen slips into place for viewing glass or tissue stereo views, designed to hold 72 views back to back, brass plaque on front w/patent dates of April 7, 1857, March 1 & 29, 1859, April 12, 1859 & December 13, 1859, America, 18 1/2" h. (ILLUS.) **1,900**

Alexander Beckers Tabletop Stereoscope

Beckers (Alexander) tabletop stereoscope, holding approximately 46 stereo views, plaque has patent dates between July and December 1859, New York, 8 1/2 x 9", 15" h. (ILLUS.) **950**

Beckers (Alexander) tabletop stereoscope, upright rosewood veneer case w/small brass plaque w/patent dates from 1857 through 1859, interior belt, optics & exterior all in very fine condition, designed to hold 36 standard size glass, flat mount or paper stereo views, America, ca. 1859, 18 1/2" h. **1,700**

Beckers Floor-standing Stereoscope

Beckers floor-standing stereoscope, rosewood veneer, brass plate on front has patent dates of "April 7th 1857, March 1st & 29th 1859, April 12th 1859 and December 13th 1859," designed to hold 144 stereo views in wire holders, frosted glass diffusing screen at back allows glass or tissue stereo views to be seen w/transmitted light (back lit), also suitable for standard card stereo views, America, ca. 1860, 16" sq. at base, 49" h. (ILLUS.) **6,500**

Beckers floor-standing stereoscope, rosewood veneer case & tall base, small brass plate on front w/patent dates from 1857 through 1859, lenses at front & back of viewer, rear lens can be removed so that glass or tissue stereo views can be viewed, designed to hold 288 stereo views in 144 wire holders, on a squared upright base w/serpentine sides & projecting rounded corners, good optics & belt & lever focusing device, refinished, overall excellent condition, America, ca. 1860, base 16" sq., 49" h. **5,500**

Beckers "Sweetheart" Stereoscope

Beckers "Sweetheart" tabletop stereoscope, cherry veneer w/rickrack trim, double capacity, w/lenses either side so that 48 views can be stored & viewed back to back, America, ca. 1859, 10 x 12" at base, 14 1/2" h. (ILLUS.) **605**

Beckers Tabletop Stereoscope

Beckers "Sweetheart" tabletop stereoscope, rosewood veneer, designed to hold 50 views stored back to back for viewing from both sides, ca. 1859, 9 1/4 x 10 3/4", 15" h. (ILLUS.) **1,200**

1860s Beckers Stereoscope

Beckers tabletop stereoscope, wooden, unusual design, ca. 1860s (ILLUS.) **1,200-1,800**

Beckers-style English Stereoscope

Beckers-style stereoscope, lovely figured mahogany graining on vertical cabinet, w/sliding box-style focusing method, two brackets on either side indicate it once had cantilevered sconces, holding about 100 stereo view cards in the standard size, on a continuous belt, ivory label identified Negretti & Zambra as maker or retailer, a couple of cards missing, some balsaming on the right lens, England, ca 1860, base 11 x 12", overall 34" h. (ILLUS.)............................... **1,700**

Binocular-style Stereoscope

Binocular-style   stereoscope,   for 45 x 107mm glass views, black finish, comes w/73 miscellaneous views, Germany, 1920s (ILLUS.) **200**

Lovely French Walnut Stereoscope

Beckers-style tabletop stereoscope, fine upright walnut case, glass diffusing screen in rear makes this suitable for glass, tissue or paper stereo views, reflecting mirror under lid directs the light to the views, both focusing & interocular adjustment, excellent optics, designed to hold 50 stereo views of the standard 3 1/4 x 7" size, case w/carved wreath under viewer lens, beveled & reeded corners, minor age crack in back, France, ca. 1880s, 10 x 11 1/2", 20" h. (ILLUS.) **3,750**

Beckers-style tabletop stereoscope, upright maple case, independent focusing lens panels on either side, holds 44 individual views in 22 double-sided holders, probably unique, America, mid-19th c., 10 x 13", 16" h. (some minor restoration) **1,200**

Box-style Stereoscope

Box-style   stereoscope,   walnut,   for 6 x 13cm glass or paper stereo views, rack & pinion focusing mechanism, ca. 1910-20s (ILLUS.).. **325**

Brewster-style Folding Stereoscope

Brewster-style folding-box stereoscope, green cloth covering, folded closed resembles a small cigar box, when opened the lens panel pops up, for standard size paper or glass views, cloth worn in a few spots but overall excellent condition, France, ca. 1870s (ILLUS.) **273**

Brewster-style stereo viewer, dark green imitation leather, unusual sliding box-type focusing arrangement, probably sold by Anthony, America, ca. 1860s, excellent condition **325**

Finely Grained Wood Stereoscope

Brewster-style stereoscope, beautifully grained hardwood case w/ogee sides, oversized metal-framed lens on the top, smoothly operating focusing mechanism, excellent condition, ca. 1870s (ILLUS.) **425**

Fine English Brewter-style Stereoscope

Brewster-style stereoscope, binocular-type focusing wheel, fine burled mahogany cabinet w/an ebony lens panel & leather-covered lens barrels, exterior in matching burl w/brass inlay, the interior of similar wood w/a compartment for the viewer as well as sections for glass & paper stereo views, excellent optics, the box w/lock & key, England, ca. 1870, box 8 x 14", 6" h. (ILLUS.) **1,870**

American Brewster-style Stereo Viewer

Brewster-style stereo viewer, upright tapering case in dark blue leather w/gold embossing, undoubtedly by Appleton of New York City, excellent condition, ca. 1860s (ILLUS.) **733**

Classic Brewster-style Stereoscope

Brewster-style stereoscope, basic design (ILLUS.) **110**

Brewster-style Mahogany Stereoscope

Brewster-style Stereoscope with Matching Box for Stereo Views

Brewster-style stereoscope, burled mahogany tapering upright case, the corners inlaid w/lighter wood, ebonized lens panels, excellent condition, ca. 1870 (ILLUS. previous page).. **500**

Brewster-style stereoscope, burled mahogany, w/matching lockable storage box w/four interior sections for stereo views, ca. 1865, the box w/key & measuring 8 1/4 x 10", 4 1/4" h. (ILLUS. top of page) **484**

Antoine Claudet Stereoscope

Brewster-style stereoscope, by Antoine Claudet, push/pull focusing brass eyepieces w/interocular adjustment, reflecting lid w/silver colored paper instead of mirrored glass, ivory plaque indicates 107 Regent Street address of Claudet in London, ca. 1855, possibly earlier (ILLUS.)...................... **600**

Brewster-style stereoscope, by Carpenter & Westley, tapering rectangular grained mahogany case w/inlaid ivory company label, early push/pull focusing

brass lens barrels, excellent condition, England, ca. 1856 .... **850**

English Brewster-style Stereoscope

Brewster-style stereoscope, grained mahogany w/ebony eyepieces, center wheel, binocular-style focusing mechanism, England, ca. 1870s (ILLUS.) **475**

Brewster-style Grained Stereoscope

Brewster-style stereoscope, grained wood w/center wheel focusing mechanism, gilt embossed leather retailer's label for Husbands of Bristol, England, ca. 1870s (ILLUS.) **475**

Stereoscope in Storage Box

Brewster-style stereoscope, in mahogany storage box, the box w/dividers for paper stereo views & another section for glass views or stereo Daguerreotypes, the interior w/original green velvet lining, original key (ILLUS.) **800**

Wooden Brewster-style Stereoscope

Brewster-style stereoscope, light pine colored wood, England or France (ILLUS.) **643**

Mahogany Brewster-style Stereoscope

Brewster-style stereoscope, mahogany, classic tapering rectangular design, overall excellent condition, mid-19th c. (ILLUS.)........ **425**

Stereoscope on Ornate Brass Column

Brewster-style stereoscope, mahogany on ornate brass/gilt column, rack & pinion focusing by knurled brass knob underneath viewer, England, ca. 1856, original reflecting mirror slightly de-silvered at edges, about 15" h. (ILLUS.)..................... **1,100**

*London Stereoscopic
Brewster-style Stereoscope*

Brewster-style stereoscope, mahogany, w/brass-barreled eyepieces, sliding interocular lens panel & push/pull focusing, ivory plaque on underside reads "London Stereoscopic Company, 313 Oxford St.," England, ca. 1855 (ILLUS.) **345**

Napoleon III-style Stereoscope

Brewster-style stereoscope, Napoleon III-style, highly decorated case, ebony lens barrel, center wheel focusing mechanism, France, 1870s-80s (ILLUS.) **500**

Decorative Brewster-style Stereoscope

Brewster-style stereoscope, Napoleon III-style, scroll-decorated case w/ogee sides, oversized optics & center wheel focusing mechanism, France, 1870s-80s (ILLUS.) **1,500**

Stereoscope on Adjustable Stand

Brewster-style stereoscope, on adjustable brass stand, sliding box-type focusing, ivory label reading "C.W. Dixey" (important opticians in London in the 1860s-70s), completely detaches from stand for use as hand viewer, ca. 1860, 17" extending to 23" h. (ILLUS.) **1,133**

Stereoscope on Turned Mahogany Stand

Brewster-style stereoscope, on turned mahogany stand, w/ivory retailer's label reading "C.W. Dixey - Opticians to the Queen - 3 New Bond Street, London," ca. 1860, 15" h. (ILLUS.) **1,210**

Stereoscope of Papier-mâché

Brewster-style stereoscope, papier-mâché w/gilding & mother-of-pearl inlay, probably America, ca. 1860, mirror under reflecting lid is replacement (ILLUS.) **4,000**

English Brewster-style Pine Stereoscope

Brewster-style stereoscope, rare light pine wood case, brass barreled eyepieces sight from side to side for interocular adjustment, England, mid-19th c., overall excellent condition (ILLUS.) **600**

Unusual Tin Ware Stereoscope

Brewster-style stereoscope, tin ware, unusual primitive style by unknown manufacturer, America, ca. 1860s (ILLUS.).......... **350**

Unusually Shaped Early Stereoscope

Brewster-style stereoscope, upright wooden case w/ogee sides, smooth rack & pinion focusing mechanism, France or England, very tiny age crack in corner of reflecting lid, overall excellent condition, ca. 1860s (ILLUS.)....................... **400**

Brewster-style stereoscope, w/center wheel focusing mechanism, France or England, ca. 1870s, original mirror under reflecting lid w/some desilvering doesn't affect operation (ILLUS. also on top of next page) **350**

Stereoscope with Original Box

Brewster-style stereoscope, w/rack & pinion focusing, in original box, France, ca. 1880s (ILLUS.) **700**

Brewster-style Stereoscope

*Brewster-style Stereoscope
on Turned Pedestal*

Brewster-style stereoscope, walnut, on turned pedestal stand, America, ca. 1870s (ILLUS.) **800-1,200**

Brewster-style stereoscope, wood graining, center wheel focusing works smoothly, optics are first rate, England, ca. 1860s, minor loss of silver from mirror underneath reflecting lid (ILLUS.) **300**

Brewster-style Stereoscope on Base

Brewster-style stereoscope on adjustable turned wood base, w/large diameter lens w/excellent optics, very smooth focusing mechanism, France or England, second half 19th c., overall excellent condition, 14" h. extending to 20" h. (ILLUS.) . **1,730**

Brewster-style stereoscope on matching turned wood column, walnut case, top loading-style, scope lifts easily off the column to become handheld, excellent condition w/tiny repair where viewer joins stand, America, ca. 1860s, 14" h. **600**

English Brewster-style Stereoscope

Cadwell Stereoscope

Cadwell Revolving Stereoscope, horizontal octagonal form, walnut frame, holds 100 views back to back, patented January 6, 1874, J.W. Cadwell, United States, overall excellent condition (small chip of wood missing from the lens housing)........ **1,800**

Cadwell revolving stereoscope, wooden, J.W. Cadwell, United States, ca. 1870s (ILLUS. bottom previous column) ... **1,200-1,500**

Scarce Octagonal Revolving Stereoscope

Cadwell revolving stereoscope, walnut, octagonal, holds 100 views back to back, w/lock & key, patented Jan. 6, 1874, J.W. Cadwell, United States (ILLUS.) **2,500**

Cadwell Octagonal Stereoscope

Cadwell stereoscope, octagonal wooden case, lens assembly swings to either side to allow viewing of stereo cards from both sides, push-pull device to allow focusing for each view, small chip & small age crack in case, patented January 3, 1874, J.W. Cadwell, United States (ILLUS.) **1,400**

Cadwell stereoscope, walnut, w/diffused glass in top lid, double-sided, designed to hold 96 stereo views back to back so that images can be viewed from either side, J.W. Cadwell, United States, 9 1/4 x 12", 12" h. (ILLUS. top of page) **1,700**

"Camerascope" stereo viewer, black metal, folding type, in original box, comes w/two complete sets of 12 views, ca. 1930s (ILLUS. top of next page) **55**

"Camerascope" viewer, folding-type, in original worn box & w/a complete set of 24 stereo pairs of cigarette cards titled "Peeps Into Many Lands," excellent condition, England, ca. 1930s, the set (ILLUS. top of page 121) **146**

Cadwell Revolving Stereoscope

"Camerascope"
Stereo Viewer

Carpenter & Westley Stereoscope

Carpenter & Westley stereoscope, wooden, Brewster-style, England, ca. 1856 (ILLUS.)... **700-900**

w/space for viewer & quantity of views, England, ca. 1858, 6 x 9", 5" h. (ILLUS.) .. **2,500**

Coin-op "Camera Chief" Stereoscope

Coin-op "Camera Chief" stereoscope, metal w/colorful graphics, crude advance mechanism allowing views of nine stereo transparencies of striptease "artistes" for 1 cent, 1950s, 6 x 12", 8 1/2" h. (ILLUS.)..... **399**

Swan Patent "Clairvoyant" Stereoscope

"Clairvoyant" stereoscope, Swan patent, mahogany box & view, the view w/original dark blue velvet trim, the fitted box

Rare Coin-Op Musical Stereoscope

*"Camerascope"
Viewer & Cigarette
Cards*

Coin-operated musical stereoscope, upright mahogany case w/label of Henri Vidcudez, Ste. Croix, probably designed for Swiss coins but works w/U.S. 1-cent coins, plays four different tunes while interior chain revolves the stereo views, holds 17 stereo views, frosted glass panel in the top lets light in for viewing, original key for the top front lock, overall excellent condition, ca. 1890, base 14 1/2 x 18", overall 20" h. (ILLUS. previous page) **8,000**

"Cooke Patent" Stereoscope

"Cooke Patent" stereoscope, mahogany, by the London Stereoscopic Company, patent refers to a pair of interior supplementary lenses that are swung into place by a brass knob on the left of the viewer, view w/both an "LSC" ivory plaque & a separate patent plaque in ivory, in fitted mahogany box w/compartment for ste-

reoscope & three other sections for stereo views, overall excellent condition, England, ca. 1860, box 8 x 13", 5" h. (ILLUS. previous column) **1,200**

Collapsible Stereoscope from France

Collapsible stereoscope, covered in dark green diced pattern cloth, standard size, France, ca. 1880s, folds flat to 4 x 7", 1 1/4" h.(ILLUS.) **220**

Damoy (Jules) stereoscope, box-style folding-type, a low rectangular light- colored wood box, fold-down viewer held in place by sliding lid, lid also doubling as the card holder, slipping back & forth for focusing, designed to view stereo postcards & standard stereo views w/thin mounts, excellent condition, France, early 20th c. **450**

Deluxe Holmes Bates-style Stereoscope

Deluxe Holmes Bates-style stereoscope, mahogany & figured brass, by J. Lizars, Glasgow, Scotland, rack & pinion focusing mechanism for view holder, rare, ca. 1890s (ILLUS.) **350**

Diascope Viewer for Autochromes

Diascope viewer, used for Autochromes, cloth-covered wood fold-up type, a sliding drawer in the base to store additional images, comes w/an Autochrome of a cute young girl in a garden, couple of light bends to the cardboard supporting struts, early 20th c., closed case 7 1/2" sq., 2 1/4" h. (ILLUS. open) **375**

Unidentified Early Stereoscope

Early wooden stereoscope, very simple design, marked "Patent Applied For" but unidentified (ILLUS.) **95**

"Educa" Stereoscope with Plaques

"Educa" tabletop stereoscope, manufactured by Mattey for the French school system, for 6 x 8" plaques, each w/12 stereo pairs, w/cabinet below w/space for 42 plaques, comes w/491 plaques, unusual, 8 x 10 1/2" at base, 18" h. (ILLUS.) **1,265**

Ensign "Snapscope," folding model, a concave mirror used for magnifying photographs, gives pseudo-stereoscopic effect, excellent condition in original box, ca. 1930s **75**

Ernemann Tabletop Stereoscope

Ernemann tabletop stereoscope, tall upright case w/rack & pinion focusing mechanism, interocular adjustment & internal bellows behind the lens panels, fine optics, w/one cassette for holding 20 views, for 45 x 107mm glass views, excellent condition, Germany, ca. 1930, case 5 1/2 x 6 1/2", 16" h. (ILLUS.)........... **1,200**

English Floor-standing Stereoscope

Ferris Wheel-style Photo Viewer

Ferris Wheel-style photo viewer, magnifying eyepiece, w/20 images of Venice & Milan measuring approximately 1 x 1", red paint w/gold-colored pinstriping, unusual, ca. 1900, 8" h. (ILLUS.) **425**

"Fitaskop" stereoscope, small rectangular metal case w/fold-out back, for 45 x 107mm paper or glass views, small patch of rust on top of lens panel & eyepieces, in original box, ca. 1930s (ILLUS. bottom of page) **55**

Floor-standing stereoscope, burled mahogany, holds about 200 stereo views, w/a reflecting mirror under the lid to reflect light onto the views, ground glass screen at rear, smooth sliding box-style/rack method w/excellent optics, England, ca. 1860s, small strip of veneer missing from interior of lid, 12 x 12", 48" h. (ILLUS.) **4,000-6,000**

Small Folding "Fitaskop" Stereoscope

German Folding Metal Stereoscope

Folding metal stereoscope, for film transparencies, probably premium or sales aid, designed to hold quantity of views that are moved into viewing position by turning knurled knob on right of viewer, comes w/one 3 1/4 x 4 1/4" transparency of close-up of factory machinery, Germany, ca. 1930s, company logo worn off, 6 1/4 x 5 x 1 3/4" closed (ILLUS.) **150**

French Floor-standing Stereoscope

Floor-standing stereoscope, Eastlake cabinet style, ebony veneer w/incised carving on body of viewer & gilded bronze handles on each side, glass diffusing screen on rear of viewer, designed to hold about 200 glass, tissue or paper stereo views, France, ca. 1870s, 12" sq. at base, 48" h. (ILLUS.)............................ **4,000**

French Folding Stereoscope

Folding stereoscope, black cloth-covered box, lid opens & a Brewster-style viewer automatically pops into place, France, ca. 1880s, box closed 4 x 7 1/4", 1 1/2" h. (ILLUS. open) **200**

Metal Folding Stereoscope & Views

Folding stereoscope, black metal, w/seven packets each containing ten stereo views of San Francisco & nearby areas, good quality images measuring 3 1/4 x 4 1/2", ca. 1930s, the group (ILLUS.) **130**

Folding Stereoscope & Roll of Views

Folding stereoscope, plastic, comes w/42 tinted real photo stereo views of Venice on continuous roll, in original box, ca. 1950s (ILLUS.) **225**

English Leather Folding Viewer

Folding viewer, maroon leather w/matching slipcase, England, ca. 1855 (ILLUS.) **100**

Folding viewer & stereo views, black metal, w/complete set of 24 pairs of English cigarette cards, "Peeps Into Many Lands - Third Series," ca. 1930s (ILLUS. top of next page) **73**

Ca. 1910 French Stereoscope

French stereoscope, for 6 x 13cm glass or paper stereo views, ca. 1910 (ILLUS.)......... **275**

French Gaumont Stereoscope

Gaumont stereoscope, black leather case w/viewers on the top, fine optics w/interocular focusing mechanism, for 6 x 13cm glass stereo views, France, ca. 1910 (ILLUS.).. **400**

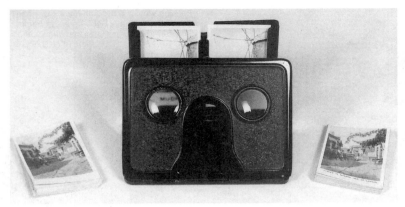

Black Metal Folding Viewer & Views

Gaumont Tabletop Stereo Viewer

Gaumont tabletop stereo viewer, for 45 x 107mm glass slides, comes w/some slides & three magazines, each to hold 20 slides, France, ca. 1920s, 8 x 10" at base, 15" h. (ILLUS.)................................. **2,500**

General Motors Multi-Vue Viewer

General Motors Multi-Vue Stereoscope, original blue leatherette case, w/view cards showing various Chevrolet model cars for 1954, used by GM dealers to promote sales, each card w/six stereo pairs, 25 cards all (ILLUS.) **500**

Gibbons patent "cigar box" stereoscope, doubles as storage box, W.J. Gibbons, England, ca. 1860, 4 x 7 1/2", 1 1/2" h. closed (ILLUS. top of page 128) **550**

Gibbons Folding Stereoscope

Gibbons patent "cigar box" stereoscope, doubles as storage box when closed, W.J. Gibbons, England, ca. 1860, 4 1/4 x 7 3/4", 2 1/4" h. closed (ILLUS.)....... **275**

Gibbons patent "cigar box" stereoscope, folding viewer, the lens panel folding flat into a box that also holds about 15 views, the lid w/photographic illustration of English country house, W.J. Gibbons, England, ca. 1860 (ILLUS. bottom of next page) **193**

Gibbons patent patent stereoscope, folding-type, shallow rectangular "cigar box" form w/viewer folding into the storage box, W.J. Gibbons, England, ca. 1860, closed 4 x 7 1/2", 1 1/4" h. **300**

Gibbons English Patent Stereoscope

Gibbons patent stereoscope, unusual open design for the simple wooden frame, illustrates transition from the Brewster style to the Holmes-Bates design, W.J. Gibbons, England, ca. 1860, excellent condition (ILLUS.) **350**

French Graphoscope with Art Views

Graphoscope, fold-up type in shallow box, embossed "L'Art Pour Tous - Salon de 1891," contains 24 printed reproductions of various paintings, France, 1890s, excellent condition (ILLUS.) **80**

Derby Silver Company Graphoscope

Graphoscope, quadruple silver plate, w/6" d. magnifying lens, Derby Silver Company, Derby, Connecticut, ca. 1900-10, 15 1/2" h. (ILLUS.) **1,100**

Graphoscope, small box-form folding model for viewing cartes-de-visite, by Mattey, France, ca. 1900, excellent condition, closed 3 1/2 x 5 1/4", 1 1/4" h. **185**

*Gibbons
"Cigar Box"
Stereoscope*

Gibbons Patent Stereoscope

"Helioplast" Folding Stereoscope

"Helioplast" folding stereoscope, w/14 litho stereo views of Jerusalem, scarce, Germany, ca. 1900 (ILLUS.) **450**

American Patented Stereoscope

Holmes-Bates-style stereoscope, patented by A. Quirilo, November 12, 1872, America, excellent condition (ILLUS.) **250**

Holmes-Bates-style Stereoscope

Holmes-Bates-style stereoscope, patented by A. Quirilo, November 12, 1872, variant of Quirilo viewers, America (ILLUS.) **275**

Holmes-Bates-style Stereoscope

Holmes-Bates-style stereoscope, bird's-eye maple w/original velvet liner around eye hood, marked "The Paragon Scope Keystone View Co." (ILLUS.) **65**

American Holmes-Bates-style Stereoscope

Holmes-Bates-style stereoscope, patented by A. Quirilo, October 27, 1874, completely detaches from stand, handle fits firmly into socket at top of stand, America, 14" h. (ILLUS.) **1,000**

American-made Stereoscope on Stand

Holmes-Bates-style stereoscope on stand, metal viewer frame w/adjustable wooden view holder, on a turned wood stand, brass flange on bottom of viewer marked "J.A. & Co. Patent Novbr. 12, 1877," very slight wear to edges of hood, America, 1870s (ILLUS.) **190**

Holmes-Bates-style Stereoscope on Base

Holmes-Bates-style stereoscope on base, scrolled metal legs support the turned wood support pedestal, detaches for handheld use, small chip to wood, hood w/some minor restoration, America, ca. 1890s (ILLUS.) **535**

Stereoscope in Finely Carved Box

Holmes-Bates-style stereoscope & storage box, the stereoscope hood w/fine gilt decoration, adjustable wood view holder, in a finely crafted original fitted hardwood box, the rectangular top lid deeply incised w/scrolls & crosses centered by the large script wood "Stereoscope," the front edge centered by a large incised "M," interior w/two sections to hold views, one latch missing from front of box, overall excellent condition, America, ca. 1870, box 6 1/2 x 13 1/2", 4 1/2" h. (ILLUS.) **900**

"Imperial" Novelty Stereoscope

"Imperial" novelty stereoscope, folding-type, Art Nouveau designed metal frame, by the Rotograph Company, New York, New York, three-fold design w/colorful graphics, comes w/20 miniature stereo views, ca. 1900, very slight overall wear, views measure 1 x 2" (ILLUS.)..................... **170**

Ives "Kromskop" tabletop stereoscope, uses special triple glass slides for a color effect, first & only stereo viewer specifically designed for the additive color process, patented December 18, 1894, minimal signs of wear, original hood missing but a facsimile hood & two Kromogram slides included (ILLUS. top of next page)... **1,650**

Kershaw & Sons Stereoscope

Kershaw & Sons stereoscope, marked "Kershaw & Sons, Ltd., Leeds 1918, Stereoscope No. 1, Mk 1, No. 584," unusual, England (ILLUS.)... **425**

Keystone Junior 1933 Stereoscope

Keystone Junior stereoscope, maroon-colored case, in the original box labeled "Keystone Third Dimension Photographs and Stereoscope - Chicago World's Fair 1933," includes 20 various stereo views of the fair, each measuring 2 1/2 x 4 3/4", one view creased, otherwise excellent condition, Keystone View Company, United States, the set (ILLUS.) **350**

Keystone Salesman's Sample Kit

Keystone "Monarch Stereoscope" sales-man's sample kit, includes the stereoscope & "Manual of Instruction - For the Use of Salesmen of the Keystone View Company," in original leatherette carrying case, dated 1903, slight wear on case, Keystone View Company, United States, the set (ILLUS.)............................... **600**

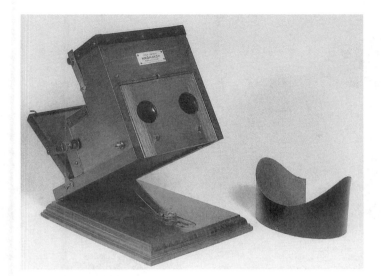

*Rare Ives
"Kromskop"
Color Viewer*

Late Keystone Stereoscope

Keystone stereoscope, mounted on a wooden easel & fitted w/an electric light at the top, includes two sets of eye test stereo views & a booklet on binocular vision, excellent optics, excellent condition, Keystone View Company, United States, ca. 1940 (ILLUS.)............................ **302**

Keystone "Telebinocular" Stereoscope

Keystone "Telebinocular" stereoscope, on adjustable metal stand w/electric light, needs rewiring, Keystone View Company, United States (ILLUS.) **242**

"Telebinocular" Stereoscope on Stand

Keystone "Telebinocular" stereoscope, on stand, America, ca. 1920s, slight wear to eyepiece, Keystone View Company, United States, 12" h. adjusting to 16" h. (ILLUS.) **180**

Art Deco Keystone "Telebinocular" Stereoscope

Keystone Telebinocular stereoscope, on stand, Art Deco style, w/a black crinkle finish, viewer & adjustable view holder on an adjustable metal stand, excellent condition, Keystone View Company, United States, ca. 1930s (ILLUS.) **600**

Keystone "Televiewer" stereoscope, handheld model in Art Deco style, slight wear to blue crackle finish, in the original storage box made to look like a pair of books, Keystone View Company, United States, ca. 1930s, overall excellent condition.. **170**

Knight's "Cosmorama" Stereoscope

Knight's "Cosmorama" stereoscope, mahogany grain & ornate scrollwork hinges w/enamel inlay, on barley twist column, the view w/sliding box-style focusing arrangement, the front lens panel dropping down for cleaning inside of lenses, rare, George Knight, England, ca. 1855, 11 3/4" h. (ILLUS.) **3,750**

Knight's "Cosmorama" stereoscope on pedestal base, rosewood case w/brass connecting arm to the right side, arm connected to the mirrored reflecting lid on the top to the rear door, enables smooth transition when viewing back-tinted tissue views, suitable for standard flat mount, paper or glass views, overall excellent condition, on a barley-twist column above a round disk base, rare, George Knight, England, ca. 1854, overall 16 1/2" h. **3,250**

"Kodaslide" Stereo Viewer II in Box

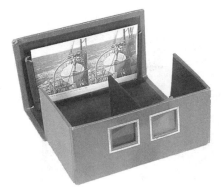

"La Stereo Carte" Stereoscope

Kodak "Kodaslide" Stereo Viewer II, in fitted velvet box, extension wire & new electrical connecting plug added to original (ILLUS.) **65**

Kodak "Kodaslide" Stereo Viewer II

Kodak "Kodaslide" Stereo Viewer II, mint condition in original box, ca. 1950s (ILLUS.) **100**

"La Stereo Carte" stereoscope, cardboard, folding box style, designed for stereo postcards, w/packet of 24 stereo postcards of Mediterranean ports, France, ca. 1920, 7 x 4 x 3 1/2" (ILLUS. top of page) **100**

"La Stereo Carte" stereoscope, unusual folding variety, designed to view French stereo postcards, comes w/two scarce complete sets of 12 stereo postcards, France, ca. 1900 (ILLUS. bottom of page) **193**

"Le Merveilleux" stereoscope, folding wooden case, lens panel folds flat, for viewing stereo postcards, comes w/a pack of 12 stereo postcards of the Gavarnie region of France, made in France, ca. 1910, excellent condition, 4 x 6", 4" h. (ILLUS. top of next page) **266**

"Le Minimus" multiple stereoscope, for 45 x 107mm glass slides, w/10 glass slides, France, ca. 1907, excellent condition, 5 x 5", 6" h. **1,600**

French "La Stereo Carte" Stereoscope

"Le Merveilleux" Stereo Postcard Viewer

"Le Taxiphote" Stereoscope

"Le Taxiphote" stereoscope, by Jules Richard, for 45 x 107mm glass stereo views, the crank handle on the left side automatically advancing the magazine to show the next view, comes w/one magazine to hold 25 views, includes 19 glass stereo views of World War I, France, ca. 1920, 9 x 9 1/2 x 10" (ILLUS.)...................... **726**

"Lee Patent" stereo-graphoscope, 2 1/4" d. magnifying lens, ca. 1870s, 5 1/2 x 10" at base (ILLUS. top of left column, next page) **374**

"Le Multiphote" Cabinet Stereoscope

"Le Multiphote" cabinet stereoscope, for 45 x 107mm glass stereo slides, the slides stored in top tray, then dropping down to viewing position as the tray is brought forward, then into storage tray at the bottom, center wheel focusing mechanism, w/approximately 18 slides, France, ca. 1913, 5 1/2 x 6 1/2", 9" h. (ILLUS.).. **1,100**

"Lee Patent" Stereo-Graphoscope

"Lee Patent" stereo-graphoscope, collapsible-style, ebonized wood w/bone handles & finials, viewer w/large round magnifying lens above the stereo lenses, a drawer in the base to store views, ca. 1870s, opens to 16" h., box closed 7 x 11" (only slight wear to ebony) **1,000**

"Lee Patent" Walnut Stereo-Graphoscope

"Lee Patent" stereo-graphoscope, walnut, 2 1/4" d. magnifying lens, America, ca. 1870s, 5 1/2 x 10" base, 11 1/5" h. fully extended (ILLUS.) **375**

"Lee Patent"
Stereo-Graphoscope with Hinged Top

"Lee Patent" stereo-graphoscope, rectangular hardwood base w/hinged top fitted w/stereo lens & large magnifying lens for cabinet cards or cartes-de-visite, excellent condition, ca. 1870s, 7 x 10", 14" h. (ILLUS.) **707**

1870s "Lee Patent" Stereo-Graphoscope

"Lee Patent" stereo-graphoscope, walnut, top viewer section folds out from rectangular base, ca. 1870s, small sliver of wood missing from base, otherwise excellent condition (ILLUS.) **275**

Lewis (W.H.) casket stereo-graphoscope, mahogany, 6 1/2" d. magnifying lens, ca. 1876, 13 1/2 x 15 1/2", 6 1/2" h. closed, opens to 26" l. & 22" h. (ILLUS. top of next page) **2,000**

Lewis (W.H.) stereo-graphoscope, casket-style, rectangular wooden case unfolds to present scroll-cut stereo view holder, American-made, patented July 6, 1874, case base 12 x 14" closed (ILLUS. bottom of next page) **2,250**

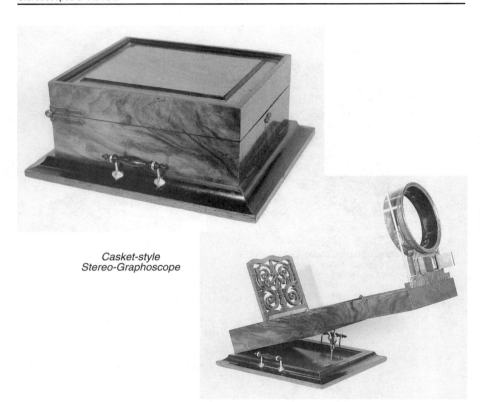

*Casket-style
Stereo-Graphoscope*

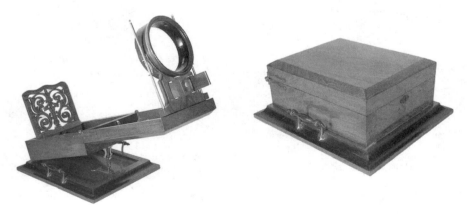

Fine Lewis Casket Stereo-Graphoscope

Rare Ebony Lewis Stereoscope on Stand

Lewis (W.H.) stereoscope on stand, ebony turned stand w/wide round base & center pedestal supporting the stereoscope, patented June 14, 1881, one of the ivory or bone finials is a replacement, once probably had a detachable magnifying glass, rare design (ILLUS.) **550**

Tabletop Stereoscope on Adjustable Brass Column

London Stereoscopic Co. tabletop stereoscope, on adjustable brass column, suitable for viewing glass or paper stereo views in standard size, w/rack & pinion focusing & interocular adjustment, probably made in France, ca. 1910, 25" h. fully extended (ILLUS.) **650**

Lorgnette-style Stereoscope

Lorgnette-style stereoscope, nickel plated, complete w/ten 45 x 107mm stereo views, rare, France, ca. 1910 (ILLUS.) **350**

Early Lorgnette-style Stereoscope

Lorgnette-style stereoscope, probably a Jules Dubosc Patent design, marked w/retail blind stamp of W.E. & F. Newton, Opticians and Globe Makers in London, slight signs of use but excellent condition, ca. 1855 (ILLUS.) **500**

Fine "Mascher's Improved Stereoscope"

"Mascher's Improved Stereoscope," Philadelphia, patented March 8, 1853, quarter-plate size, rectangular narrow

*Metropolitan
Syndicate Press
Miniature Stereoscope*

folding case, opens for stereo viewing of
an Ambrotype of a man seated next to a
table, ca. 1850s (ILLUS.) **1,400**

Rosewood Patented Stereoscope

**Mathieu (François) patented stereo-
scope,** rosewood, folding style, patented
Feb.   8,   1858,   England,
2 3/4 x 4 1/4 x 2 1/2" closed (ILLUS.) **550**
**"Metascope" combination stereoscopic
viewer/projector,** by Mattey, mahogany
cabinet, for stereo glass slides in
6 x 13cm format, comes w/one magazine
& 15 glass stereo slides, scarce,
France, ca. 1920s, missing working anaglyphic filters for projecting, 10 1/2 x 11",
16" h. (ILLUS. next column) **700**
**Military reconnaissance mirror stereo-
scope,** by the Q-O-S Corp, New York,
New York, long four-legged arched frame
w/viewer at the top center, originally designed for military use, can be used for
large stereo prints up to 8 x 8", binocular
supplementary lenses present, in fitted
wooden box, ca. 1940s (ILLUS. bottom
right) **550**

"Metascope" Stereoscopic Viewer/Projector

**Metropolitan Syndicate Press miniature
stereoscope,** green & gold metal, w/25
double-sided 1 1/2 x 3" stereo views, ca.
1907 (ILLUS. top of page)............................ **180**

Military Reconnaissance Stereoscope

Miniature Graphoscope

Miniature graphoscope for cartes de visite, 2" d. magnifying glass, comes w/group of 22 cartes of Paris, France, 3 x 5", 1" h. closed (ILLUS. top of page) **125**

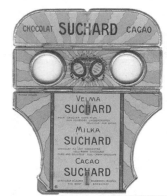

Early Hand-held Mirrorscope

Miniature Premium Stereoscope

Miniature premium stereoscope, for Suchard Chocolate & Cacao, colorful Art Deco-style tinplate, comes w/ten mini views measuring 1 1/4 x 2 3/4" (ILLUS.) **160**

Mirrorscope, hand-held model w/wooden handle & large round mirror, for viewing cartes-de-visite, cabinet cards & postcards, looking in the 8" d. convex mirror gives a pseudo-stereoscopic effect, some slight de-silvering, ca. 1890s (ILLUS.) **225**

French Monoscopic Viewer

Monoscopic viewer, upright slightly tapering rectangular wooden case w/only a few light lens scratches, together w/19 panoramic slides, two are Autochromes, the other black & white diapositive images, slides 2 5/8 x 5 1/8", France, 19th c., the group (ILLUS. of viewer) **900**

Nelson Chase Shaker stereoscope, folding-type, patented July 16, 1872, designed by Shaker Brother Nelson Chase, metal hood w/some paint flaking, adjustable wooden view holder, w/original labeled box, overall excellent condition (ILLUS. bottom of page) **3,250**

"Omnium" stereoscope, hand-held model, turned wood handle, designed to view stereoscopic postcards as well as standard size stereo views, in original storage box & w/a packet of 12 stereoscopic postcards, France, ca. 1930s, excellent condition.. **475**

Rare "Lazy Tong" Stereoscope

Page (E.K.) patent stereoscope, "lazy tong"-style, expandable metal frame between viewer & view-holding rack, turned wood handle, patented July 5, 1870, rare, excellent condition, United States (ILLUS.) **550**

Rare Nelson Chase Shaker Stereoscope

Lazy Tong-style Stereoscope

Page (E.K.) patent stereoscope, "lazy tong"-style, nickel-plated expandable frame w/turned wood handle & ebony eyepieces, patented July 5, 1870, some minor tarnishing on nickel plate, United States (ILLUS.).. **500**

Page (E.K.) patent stereoscope, unusual "lazy tong" hand-held model, gold-embossed cardboard hood, wooden handle & view rack, slide holder stamped w/patent dates of 1870 & 1878, excellent condition, United States, 1870s **425**

E.K. Page "Lazy Tong" Stereoscope

Page (E.K.) stereoscope, Holmes-Bates style, "lazy tong" viewer, embossed w/patent dates of July 5, 1870 & March 26, 1878, United States (ILLUS.) **475**

"Perfecscope" stereoscope, all-metal w/grained design, Holmes-Bates-style, by H.C. White, ca. 1910, slight pitting to metal surface & velvet trim missing from hood (ILLUS. right) **75**

E.K. Page Stereoscope

Page (E.K.) stereoscope, "lazy tong" style, w/embossed leather hood, patent dates of July 5, 1870 & March 26, 1875, some wear to edges of hood, United States (ILLUS.) **225**

Pattberg Stereoscope on Stand

Pattberg Stereoscope, viewer & view card rack raised on a nickel-plated stand w/round base, all-original, patented July 5, 1881, excellent condition, overall 12" h. (ILLUS.) **850**

Metal "Perfecscope" Stereoscope

"Perfecscope" in Oak Cabinet

"Perfecscope" stereoscope, bird's-eye maple, Holmes-Bates-style, w/50 miscellaneous Keystone cards, in oak cabinet, ca. 1900, cabinet 10 1/2 x 15 1/2", 5 3/4" h. (ILLUS.) **484**

"Photoscope" stereoscope, coin-operated w/10-cent play, clockwork mechanism works well w/excellent optics, shows five different sets of photographic stereo views, comes w/winding key for the mechanism & locking key for the door, includes a Charlie Chaplin sequence in the viewer, few rust spots on body but overall very good condition, ca. 1920s **750**

French Planox Stereoscope

Planox Stereoscope, tabletop model, walnut or mahogany upright case on block feet & brass fittings, excellent optics, rack & pinion focusing mechanism & interocular adjustment, for 6 x 13cm glass slides, comes w/one cassette to hold 20 views, includes 19 quality glass views of Italy,

France, ca. 1920, minor imperfections, 9 1/2 x 10 1/2", 12" h. (ILLUS.) **1,200**

"Pocket Rotoscope" Stereoscope

"Pocket Rotoscope" stereoscope, w/13 miniature stereo views of London measuring 1 1/4 x 2 3/4", England, ca. 1920s (ILLUS.)... **125**

"Primus Perfect Stereoscope" on pedestal base, deep reddish brown mahogany case w/brass fittings, rack & pinion focusing & interocular device, very useful for glass & tissue as well as standard flat mount paper views, ring-turned pedestal base, England, ca. 1880-90, excellent condition, 18 1/2" h. **2,750**

Quirilo Patent Stereoscope

Quirilo (A.) patent stereoscope, wood veneer, Holmes-Bates-style, United States, ca. 1873 (ILLUS.)............................. **125**

Rare Rawson's Stereoptican

"Rawson's Stereoptican - Pat'd Jan. 22, 1867," combination stereoscope & storage box, cloth exterior of viewer somewhat stained & worn, rare, 4 1/2 x 8 1/2", 1 3/4" h. (ILLUS.) **550**

Miniature Mirror Viewer

Reflecting mirror viewer for cartes de visite & cabinet cards, miniature version of viewer w/4" d. mirror magnifying the image & giving pseudo stereoscopic effect, England, ca. 1900 (ILLUS.) **90**

Jules Richard Walnut Stereoscope

Richard (Jules) box-style stereoscope, rectangular walnut case, working rack & pinion focusing mechanism, excellent optics, includes group of six slides from World War I, for 45 x 107mm views, France, ca. 1920s (ILLUS.) **250**

Richard (Jules) stereoscope, wood, box form focusing type for 45 x 107mm glass stereo slides, comes w/36 glass slides of 1939 World's Fair in New York (ILLUS. bottom of page) **275**

Jules Richard Stereoscope

"Taxiphote" Stereoscope

Richard (Jules) "Taxiphote" stereo-scope, for 45 x 107mm glass slides, w/original electric lamp, on pedestal column, w/three drawers beneath viewer, each holding four trays, each tray able to hold 25 slides, over additional 12 drawers, each holding four trays, comes w/about 550 glass stereo views of America & Europe, wood of viewer probably refinished at some point & doesn't match wood of pedestal, lock is replacement & comes w/two keys, France, ca. 1910, overall 55" h. (ILLUS.) **2,904**

Richard (Jules) "Taxiphote" stereo-scope, for glass views in 45 x 107mm size, comes w/eight Taxiphote cassettes, each holding 25 slides of European locations, & mono projection system, France, ca. 1920s, 9 x 9 1/2", 10 1/2" h. (ILLUS. bottom of page)............................ **2,750**

Richard "Taxiphote" Stereoscope

Richard (Jules) "Taxiphote" stereo-scope, upright wooden case w/two drawers in the base, each holding four magazines w/25 slides each, celluloid counter on the sides w/a few chips, mechanical slide operation, for 6 x 13cm glass stereo slides, France, ca. 1920s, case 13" sq., 20" h. (ILLUS.) **3,250**

Two Views of the
Jules Richard "Taxiphote" Stereoscope

Photographica Gallery
Cameras

Stereoscopic field camera with additional lens board with lens for mono work, Scotland, ca. 1890s, **$1,800.**

"Sport-GebrauchsmusterSchutz - No. 1500" camera, Germany, ca. 1900, **$800.**

Folding-type Kodak No. 2 Brownie Model A camera, ca. 1904, **$85.**

Kodak Boy Scout U.S.A. Model folding camera and case with Boy Scout logo, ca. 1930, **$180.**

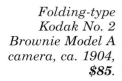

No. 1 Demon Detective camera, England, ca. 1889, **$1,500-2,500.**

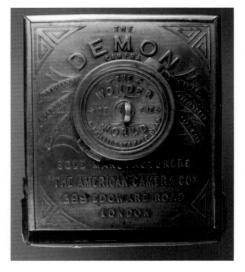

Kodak
Petite Camera
Ensemble,
includes folding camera,
compact and lipstick, all in
green suede case with mirror,
ca. 1930, $1,200.

Victo folding-type
camera by Houghton,
ca. 1900, $325.

Tintype button
camera,
ca. 1900,
$1,000-1,500.

"Cycle
Wizard" Model A
folding-type camera by the
Manhattan Optical Company
of New York City, ca. 1905, $90.

Lumiere "Sterelux"
Model 1 camera, roll
film stereo type, France,
ca. 1920s, $225.

Kodak No. 2 Hawkette camera, folding type in Bakelite case, England, ca. 1930s, $99.

Monobloc stereo camera by Jeaneret & Cie., Paris, France, ca. 1920s, $250.

Daguerreotype camera in chamfered box, ca. 1840s, $12,000-15,000.

Linex stereo camera and viewer outfit, all in original cardboard box with case and instructions, ca. 1950s, $225.

Simda Stereo Panoramascope camera, France, ca. 1955, $850-1,250 (left), and Wollensak Model 10 Stereoscopic camera, United States, ca. 1955, $450-650.

Kodak No. 3A
  Panoram
  camera, self-
  contained in case,
  ca. 1926, **$325**.

Kodak
  Brownie
  Flash B box
  camera with
  original case, ca.
  1950s, **$35**.

ICA (Zeiss) Stereo Ideal
camera folding-type
Model 650, ca. 1930, **$250**.

Ensign "Ful-Vue" camera,
England, ca. 1950s, **$50-100**.

All-metal
Photosphere
camera with
rare magazine
back, France,
ca. 1890s,
$2,500-3,500.

Sliding box wet plate camera, England, ca. 1855-65, **$2,000-3,000**.

Stereoscopic field camera, England, ca. 1880s, **$2,000-3,000**.

Camera-related

Figural "Birdie" studio distracting device, late-19th to early-20th century, **$350**.

Watkins "Bee" Meter pocket watch-style exposure meter, ca. 1900, **$75**.

Metal darkroom lantern, front embossed "Kodak," ca. 1930s, **$25**.

Stereoscopes & Viewers

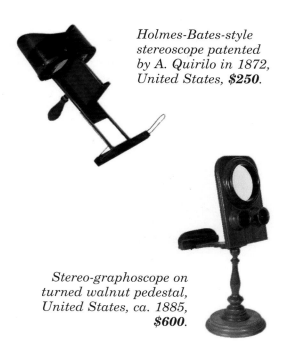

Holmes-Bates-style
stereoscope patented
by A. Quirilo in 1872,
United States, *$250*.

Coin-operated musical
stereoscope with label
of Henri Vidcudez, Ste.
Croix (Switzerland),
holds 17 stereo views,
ca. 1890, ***$8,000***.

Stereo-graphoscope on
turned walnut pedestal,
United States, ca. 1885,
$600.

Mirrorscope
for viewing
cartes-de-visite, cabinet
cards and postcards, the
convex mirror giving a
pseudo-stereoscopic effect,
ca. 1890s, ***$225.***

Stereo-graphoscope,
England or France,
ca. 1880s, ***$450-650***.

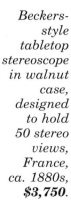

Folding stereoscope with complete set of 24 pairs of cigarette real photo stereo views, "Peeps into Prehistoric Times," published by Cavenders, 1930s, $50.

Beckers-style tabletop stereoscope in walnut case, designed to hold 50 stereo views, France, ca. 1880s, $3,750.

"The Pocket Rotoscope" miniature novelty stereoscope in folding metal case resembling a book when closed, England, 1930s, $200 (shown open and closed).

Brewster-style stereoscope with oversized metal-framed lens on top, ca. 1870s, $425.

Brewster-style stereoscope by Carpenter & Westley, England, ca. 1856, $700-900.

*Box-style stereo-
graphoscope in
mahogany case
with ebony trim,
France,
ca. 1870s,
$2,250.*

*Lewis stereoscope
on ebony turned
stand, patented
June 14, 1881,
$550.*

*Brewster
stereoscope
in mahogany
case, mid-19th
century, $425.*

*Unis
Standard
stereoscope by
Mattey, ca. 1930s, $225.*

*Planox tabletop
stereoscope on block feet,
ca. 1920, $1,200.*

*Tabletop-style stereo-graphoscope,
United States, ca. 1870s,
$250-350.*

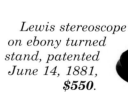

Swan's Patent Clairvoyant folding-type stereoscope in original mahogany domed-lid box, England, ca. 1858, $2,250.

Holmes-Bates-style stereoscope and storage box to hold viewer and views, United States, ca. 1870, $900 (box shown open with viewer and closed).

Smith, Beck & Beck Patent Mirror Model No. 1766 folding-type stereoscope, England, ca. 1858, $600.

Stereographoscope in folding wooden case, France, ca. 1880-1890, $550.

Floor-standing stereoscope, England, ca. 1860s, $4,000-6,000.

"TDC Stereo Vivid Viewer" in original box, ca. 1950s, $110.

Brewster-style stereoscope on turned walnut stand, United States, ca. 1870s, $800-1,200.

Nelson Chase Shaker folding-type stereoscope designed by Shaker Brother Nelson Chase, patented July 16, 1872, with original labeled box, $3,250.

R.R. Whiting's Patent 1-cent Coin-op "Sculptoscope," ca. 1922, $750.

Sibley stereoscope, United States, ca. 1870s, $2,000-3,000.

Other Objects

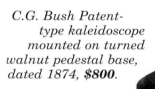

"Lanterne Medallion" magic lantern by Lapierre with upright tinplate frame, France, late 19th century, $475.

C.G. Bush Patent-type kaleidoscope mounted on turned walnut pedestal base, dated 1874, $800.

Megalethoscope by Carlo Ponti in case with ornate carved decoration, Italy, ca. 1870s, $10,500.

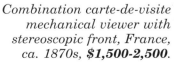

"Fantascope" set by Ackerman of London, composed of 12 animation discs and original wood and ivory handle, all in original wooden box, England, ca. 1833, $4,500.

Combination carte-de-visite mechanical viewer with stereoscopic front, France, ca. 1870s, $1,500-2,500.

Ceramic plate with black and white transfer-printed scene titled "Photographies en Costumes de Voyage," France, ca. 1890s, $100.

Stanhope in the form of a pipe, view in handle shows the Glasgow International Exhibition of 1901, $180.

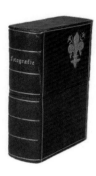

Book-shaped storage box for cabinet cards, marked in gold "Fotografie," $140.

Perspective view for a Peep Show of a Chinese temple (above) with holes and cutouts for back lighting (right), France, ca. 1800, $130.

Brass Art Nouveau-style magic lantern, ca. 1900, $400-600.

Kinora Company Ltd. animation viewer, home version of a Mutoscope in miniature, England, ca. 1912, $2,000.

"Lampadophore" magic lantern by Lapierre, France, ca. 1890s, $1,300.

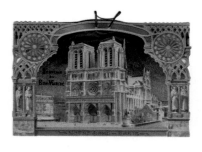

Transposing day / night view of Notre Dame Cathedral in Paris, sold by Paris department store Le Bon Marche, ca. 1890, $55 (both views shown).

Salesman's sample case of photo buttons from Cruver Mfg. Company of Chicago, with catalogs, order forms, envelopes and other ephemera, all in metal-reinforced case, ca. 1929, $400.

Photo album titled "Zeppelin-Weltfahrten," complete with 264 real bromo-silver photo cards of zeppelins and views from zeppelins, issued by German cigarette company Greilin, 1933, $275.

Kinora Company Ltd. motion picture viewer, England, ca. 1900, $2,000-2,500.

Photo Images

Autochrome of little girl, **$130**.

Ivorytype of young mother with baby, in half-leather case missing lid, 1870s, **$350**.

Ambrotype portrait of English military officer by Antoine Claudet, ca. 1855, **$1,100**.

"Robinson's Patent Photograph Album-Viewer" by D. Millard & Co. of Ohio, designed to hold about 50 cartes-de-visite on a continuous roll, stenciled on bottom "Patented April 11, 1865," **$650**.

Stereo Daguerreotype of nude seated with guitar, France, mid-19th century, **$6,500**.

Autochrome of a room interior in the French Provincial style, early-20th century, **$120**.

Autochrome of farmyard, early-20th century, $350.

Autochrome of seated woman, marked "Autochrome Lumiere," early-20th century, $200.

Cabinet Card showing Queen Victoria and her servant, John Brown, in donkey cart, by Gunn & Stewart, $110.

Autochrome of fashionable woman, 1920s, $550.

Autochrome of stained glass church window, early 20th century, $80.

Autochrome of flowers in a vase, $300.

Cabinet Card of Sarah Bernhardt in the role of Theodora, by Nadar, France, late-19th century, $200.

Daguerreotype of little girl with flowers, England, ca. 1850s, $650.

Ambrotype of young family, in full leather case, ca. 1850s, $550.

Daguerreotype of outdoor scene, resealed in full leather case, $2,000.

Ambrotype of bride in studio setting, England, 1850s, $350.

"Mascher's Improved Stereoscope" with folding case that opens for stereo viewing of Ambrotype of seated man, ca. 1850s, $1,400.

Daguerreotype of young woman in bonnet, resealed in full leather case, $600.

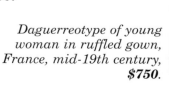

Octagonal Union case molded with a scene called "The Horse Race," mid-19th century, $500.

Daguerreotype of young woman in ruffled gown, France, mid-19th century, $750.

English Tin Novelty Viewer

Robinson's Patent Photo Album/Viewer

Robinson's Patent Photograph Album-Viewer, by D. Millard & Co., Ohio, rectangular case covered w/a pebbled finish in a paper or cloth material, stenciled mark on the bottom "Patented April 11, 1865," designed to hold about 50 cartes-de-visite on a continuous roll, four of the frames holding cards show slight damage & three are missing, one small age crack on top, w/a badly creased carte-de-visite of President Lincoln, case 5 1/4 x 9 1/2", 4 1/2" h. (ILLUS.) **650**

"Rotoscope - Folding Stereoscopic Apparatus" novelty viewer, tin, resembling book when not in use, England, 3 1/2 x 5 3/4", 3/4" h. closed (ILLUS. top of page in viewing mode) **75**

"Rowsell's Patent" Stereo-Graphoscope

"Rowsell's Patent" stereo-graphoscope, 5" d. magnifying lens, w/ivory retailer's label reading "J.H. Steward, 406 Strand, London," ivory finials, in original cardboard box w/Steward label, ca. 1870, two tiny cracks in glass screen at rear of viewer, box has been painted, 9 3/4 x 16" (ILLUS.).. **600**

*"Rowsell's Patent" Mahogany
Stereo-graphoscope*

"Rowsell's Patent" stereo-graphoscope,
nice grained mahogany adjustable frame
w/ivory finials, stereo lens & 5" d. magnifying lens for cabinet cards & cartes-de-
visite, excellent condition, ca. 1870s, ful-
ly extended 9 x 15 x 20" (ILLUS.) **550**

Scott Patent Adjustable Stereoscope

Scott patent stereoscope, fine low rectangular case on adjustable brass column,
rack & pinion focusing mechanism operated by brass knob, ivory retailer's label
for Negretti & Zambra, very fine condi-

tion, England, ca. 1856, adjusts from 15"
to 21" h. (ILLUS.) **1,900**

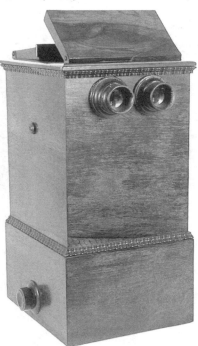

Rare Sealey & Lee Stereoscope

Sealey & Lee stereoscope, rosewood veneer, tabletop model, w/two sets of ebonized eyepieces either side of cabinet,
96 views back to back in 48 holders, interior forward & reverse belt w/winding
knobs at bottom, United States, patented March 20, 1860, rare,
9 x 10 1/2 x 18 3/4" (ILLUS.) **950**

Sibley Stereoscope

Sibley (L.D.) stereoscope, wooden, United
States, ca. 1870s (ILLUS.) **2,000-3,000**

Smith Beck & Beck Stereoscope & Cabinet

Smith Beck & Beck Achromatic Patent Stereoscope, Model No. 1071, mahogany & brass, w/original lockable matching mahogany storage cabinet designed to store viewer & views, w/key, England, ca. 1858 (ILLUS.)... **1,948**

Smith, Beck & Beck Early Stereoscope

Smith, Beck & Beck Patent Stereoscope

Smith, Beck & Beck Patent Mirror Stereoscope, Model No. 1766, folding-type, designed for viewing stereo pairs mounted in books as well as standard size glass or paper views, excellent condition, England, ca. 1858 (ILLUS.).......................... **600**

Smith, Beck & Beck No. 667 Stereoscope

Smith, Beck & Beck Patent Mirror Stereoscope, Model No. 667, originally designed for viewing stereo pairs mounted in books as well as standard size glass & paper views, w/rare original leather viewing hood (sold as accessory), ca. 1858 (ILLUS.) **1,200**

Smith, Beck & Beck Achromatic Stereoscope, Model No. 1706, upright wood cabinet storage box designed to hold both the viewer & stereo views, the additional mirrored reflecting panel included, slight sun fading to cabinet, England, ca. 1860, cabinet alone 9 x 10", 13 1/2" h. (ILLUS. left) **3,000**

Scarce Stereo Daguerreotype in Viewer

Stereo daguerreotype in viewing case, by
Newlands, Calcutta, India, in a Kilburn
fold-out viewing case dated January 12,
1853, the couple in the images identified
& having excellent contrast & sharpness,
original seal, minor wear on viewing
case, scarce example (ILLUS.) **3,500**

Stereo Daguerreotype of Gentleman

Stereo daguerreotype in viewing case,
portrait of a gentleman in unusual quarter-
plate Mascher-style viewing case, fine
quality image, excellent condition (ILLUS.) . **1,400**

Stereo Realist Green Button Stereo Viewer

**Stereo Realist Green Button stereo view-
er,** a/c electric illumination, focusing
model w/interocular & brightness
adjustment, ca. 1950s (ILLUS.) **100**

Stereo Realist Model 2062 Viewer

Stereo Realist Model 2062 viewer, green
button type w/battery adapter, mint in
original box, ca. 1950s (ILLUS.).................. **100**

English Folding Stereo Viewer

Stereo viewer, folding-type in maroon
leather, folds flat into a sleeve-type case,
probably by The London Stereoscopic
Company, some hinges reinforced where
it folds, England, ca. 1860s (ILLUS.) **120**
Stereo viewer on stand, basic Holmes-
Bates model, simulated wood hood,
wooden view holder, on turned wood
pedestal base, overall excellent condition
(some wear to hood) **125**

Folding Stereo-Graphoscope

Stereo-graphoscope, burled mahogany w/striped veneer corner trim, 5 3/4" d. magnifying glass, ca. 1880s, folds flat to 8 x 13 3/4", 3 3/4" h., opens to 20" h. (ILLUS.) **808**

Stereo-graphoscope, collapsible, folding down into self-contained box of grained mahogany inlaid w/brass & ebony banding, w/original key, both ivory finials present, uncommon, France, ca. 1870s, bottom panel carelessly re-glued, 7 3/4 x 8 3/4", 5 1/2" h. closed, 17" high in viewing position (ILLUS. bottom of page)... **950**

Fine Mahogany Stereo-Graphoscope

Stereo-graphoscope, box-style, burled mahogany w/carved ebony trim, ornate scroll carving at top of lens panel, good quality focusing mechanism & excellent optics, France, ca. 1870s, closed box 9 1/4 x 16 1/2", 5" h., opens to 22" h. (ILLUS.) **2,250**

Stereo-graphoscope, box-style collapsible model, the box w/finely grained mahogany w/inlaid brass & ebony banding, the viewer w/a large magnifying lens above the stereo lens, entire apparatus folds down into the self-contained box, uncommon style, France, ca. 1870s, opens to 19" h., box closed 8 1/2 x 9", 5 1/2" h. (ILLUS.).. **2,750**

*French
Stereo-Graphoscope*

Two Views of the Collapsible Stereo-graphoscope

Ebony Stereo-Graphoscope

Stereo-graphoscope, ebony, 5" d. magnifying lens, France, ca. 1870s, 7 x 11", 17" h. extended (ILLUS.) **275**

Stereo-graphoscope, folding-type, burl mahogany w/striped veneer corner trim, magnifying glass 5" d., folds flat to 3 x 7 x 12", excellent condition, ca. 1880s, opens to 20" h. **1,200**

Stereo-graphoscope, grained mahogany inlaid w/brass & ebony banding, collapsible type, folding down into self-contained box, very uncommon, France, ca. 1870s, 8 1/2 x 9 1/2", 51/2" h. closed, 19" h. in viewing position (ILLUS. top of page) **1,800**

French Stereo-Graphoscope

Stereo-graphoscope, folding hardwood case w/brass or nickel trim, excellent condition, France, ca. 1880-1890, base 5 3/4 x 9", extends to 14" h. (ILLUS.)........... **550**

Stereo-Graphoscope on Stand

Stereo-graphoscope, on nickel plated stand, 3 1/2" d. magnifying lens to use w/cartes de visite or cabinet cards, United States, ca. 1880s, 16 1/2" h. (ILLUS.)..... **365**

Thermo-plastic Stereo-Graphoscope

Stereo-graphoscope, unusual folding-style w/the face featuring highly embossed thermo-plastic decoration similar to material used on Union cases, magnifying lens 4" d., France, ca. 1870s, some restoration to the base but overall excellent appearance, base 7 x 11", opens to 17" h. (ILLUS.) **1,300**

Walnut Stereo-Graphoscope

Stereo-graphoscope, walnut w/ebonized lens barrels, 4 3/4" d. lens, unmarked, United States, ca. 1880s, 9 x 16", 3" h. extending to 16" h. (ILLUS.)......................... **275**

English or French Stereo-Graphoscope

Stereo-graphoscope, wooden, England or France, ca. 1880s (ILLUS.).................... **450-650**

Folding Stereoscope & View Cards

American Stereo-Graphoscope

Stereo-graphoscope, wooden, United States, ca. 1870s (ILLUS.) **250-350**

Stereo-graphoscope on stand, a turned walnut pedestal stand base supporting the device w/a large lens above the stereo lens, United States, ca. 1885, unusual design, excellent condition (ILLUS. right) **600**

Stereoscope, folding black metal type w/a complete set of 24 pairs of cigarette real photo stereo views titled "Peeps into Prehistoric Times," published by Cavenders, 1930s, the set (ILLUS. top of page) **50**

Stereoscope, folding-type, maple, fully collapsible into a self-contained cigar-style box, France, ca. 1900, box 4 x 7", 1" h. **350**

Stereoscope, so-called "cigar box" folding-type, grained mahogany case, France, ca. 1880s, closed 4 1/4 x 7 1/4", 1 1/2" h. **400**

Walnut American Stereoscope on Stand

Stereoscope, tabletop model, black ebonized wood, upright case, holds 50 glass or paper views in the standard size, France, ca. 1880, excellent condition, 10" x 10", 18" h.. **1,700**

Fine English Tabletop Stereoscope

Stereoscope, tabletop model, burled mahogany upright case, w/reflecting mirrors under the lids, ground glass in the rear to transmit light, rack & pinion sliding box-type focusing mechanism, designed to hold 25 standard size views, some skillful restoration, England, ca. 1860, 10" x 10", 13" h. (ILLUS.) **1,000**

Stereoscope, tabletop model, designed to hold 50 stereo views back to back to allow for viewing either side, rack & pinion focusing mechanism, drawer at base for additional views, America, ca. 1860s, skillful repair to bottom corner of drawer, 9 x 11", 17" h. (ILLUS. bottom of page) **2,000**

Tabletop Stereoscope on Adjustable Stand

Stereoscope, tabletop model, ebony, on adjustable stand, ca. 1890s, 15" h. (ILLUS.)... **1,100**

Tabletop Stereoscope

Ebony Tabletop Stereoscope

Stereoscope, tabletop model, ebony w/banded veneer & brass inlay, rack & pinion sliding box-style focusing mechanism, holds 50 glass or card stereo views in standard size on a chain belt, England or France, ca. 1860s, 10 1/2 x 11", 18 1/2" h. (ILLUS.) **2,500**

Fine Tabletop English Stereoscope

Stereoscope, tabletop model, fine vertical mahogany case w/early sliding box-style focusing mechanism, very well construct-ed, holds 50 stereo views, decorative & functional, England, ca. 1860s, case 10 1/4 x 11", 21 1/2" h. (ILLUS.) **1,500**

Mahogany Tabletop Stereoscope

Stereoscope, tabletop model, mahogany, early sliding box-style focusing mecha-nism, holds 50 stereo views, England, ca. 1860s, lack of bottom panel doesn't affect operation, 10 1/4 x 11" at base, 20" h. (ILLUS.)................................. **1,200**

Stereoscope in Seven-sprocket Format

Stereoscope, wooden, for 35mm slides in seven-sprocket European format, France, ca. 1950s (ILLUS.)............................ **25**

French Pocket Stereoscope

"Stereoscope de Poche" (pocket stereo-scope), folding-type, for 45 x 107mm paper or glass stereo views, viewer automatically pops up into viewing position when box is opened, comes w/box of 10 glass stereo slides, unusual, France, ca. 1910-20, 1 3/4 x 2 1/2", 5 1/2" h. closed (ILLUS.)... **275**

"Stereoscope Dixio"

"Stereoscope Dixio," using larger format print, comes w/directions, unusual, France, ca. 1900, stains, mirror needs replacing (ILLUS.) **275**

Boxed Stereoscope & Glass Slides

Stereoscope & glass slides, the focusing stereoscope in a fitted wooden box together w/30 glass stereo slides, 28 45 x 107mm glass slides of World War I battle field scenes, some very graphic, the set (ILLUS.) **425**

Stereoscope on stand, nickel-plated round base, pedestal & serpentine adjustable arms, hood recovered w/purple velvet, patented July 5, 1881, America, excellent condition (ILLUS. bottom of page) **302**

*Nickel-plated
Stereoscope on Stand*

Stereoscope & Views of World War I

French "Stereoscope L'Utile"

"Stereoscope L'Utile," maroon cardboard
  w/silver embossing, France (ILLUS.) **95**
Stereoscope & views, including 125
  45 x 107mm glass slides of World War I,
  France (ILLUS. top of page)........................ **498**

Swan's Patent Clairvoyant Stereoscope

Swan's Stereoscopic Treasury & Clairvoyant Stereoscope

Swan's Patent Clairvoyant Stereoscope, folding-type in original mahogany domed cover box, box holds viewer upside-down & also stores views, minor crack in veneer, overall excellent condition, Henry Swan, England, ca. 1858 (ILLUS.)............ **2,250**

Swan's Stereoscopic Treasury & Clairvoyant stereoscope, wooden, Henry Swan, England, ca. 1860 (ILLUS. bottom of previous page) **2,000-3,000**

Swan's "The Stereoscopic Treasury" outfit, early variant w/"Clairvoyant" stereoscope in a handsome hardwood rectangular box w/ivory label, also houses a section for storing stereo views, overall excellent condition, Henry Swan, England, ca. 1858 (red leather finger loop under viewer skillfully replaced) **1,900**

1950s "TDC Stereo Vivid Viewer" in Box

"TDC Stereo Vivid Viewer," black plastic case, for 35mm slides in Realist format, focusing & interocular adjustment, near mint in original box, ca. 1950s (ILLUS.) **110**

"The 3D Roto-Vuer" Stereoscope

"The 3D Roto-Vuer" stereoscope, boxy metal case, holds 60 Realist format stereo slides, w/instructions, battery holder & transformer in original box, near mint condition, ca. 1954 (ILLUS.) **325**

"The Camera Chief" Coin-op Stereo Viewer

"The Camera Chief" coin-op stereo viewer, w/3D cartoon of The Katzenjammer Kids, operational, w/lock & key, America, ca. 1950s, 8 x 12" at base, 10 1/2" h. (ILLUS.) **1,400**

"The Cuminoscope" Viewing Device

"The Cuminoscope" mirror viewing device for cabinet cards & cartes de visite, mahogany, a concave ebony-trimmed mirror magnifying the image & giving pseudo stereoscopic effect, ivory label w/"The Cuminoscope" & French patent, although item is of English origin, ca. 1870s, 9 3/4 x 15", 14" h. (ILLUS.) **900**

"The Pocket Rotoscope" stereoscope, miniature novelty stereoscope, folding gilt-metal case shaped like a book when closed, w/a set of 12 miniature 1 1/2" x 3 3/4" views of Liverpool, England, some pitting on case, overall very good condition, England, 1930s (ILLUS. top of next page) **200**

"The Pocket Rotoscope" Stereoscope

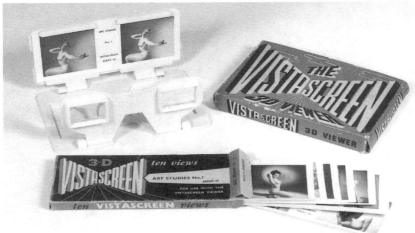

"Vistascreen 3-D Viewer" & Cards

"The Vistascreen 3-D Viewer," & Views

"Tru-Vue Deluxe 3-Dimensional Lighted Viewer"

"The Vistascreen 3-D Viewer," folding plastic viewer in original box, complete w/set of ten "Art Studios No. 1" views featuring "girlie" poses, excellent condition, 1950s, the set (ILLUS. middle of previous page) **112**

"The Vistascreen 3-D Viewer," folding plastic viewer in original worn box w/set of ten glamour girl "Art Studies No. 3," views, overall excellent condition, 1950s (ILLUS. bottom of previous page) **55**

"Tru-Vue Deluxe 3-Dimensional Lighted Viewer," black plastic hand-held model, w/12 Tru-Vue cards in sleeves, excellent condition, 1950s, the set (ILLUS. top of page) **65**

"Tru-Vue" stereoscope, plastic viewer, in original box w/four strips including 56 scenes of The Grand Canyon of Arizona, ca. 1950s, excellent condition.......... **40**

Underwood & Underwood folding stereoscope, nickel-plated metal, "lazy tong" focusing, ca. 1915 (ILLUS. bottom of page) **400**

"Unis" Folding Viewer

"Unis" folding viewer, nickel plated, for use w/standard format or stereo postcards & smaller formats, France (ILLUS.) **95**

Underwood & Underwood Folding Nickel-plated Stereoscope

Mattey 1930s "Unis" Stereoscope

"Unis" Standard Stereoscope, by Mattey, hardwood hand-held model w/smooth focusing mechanism & interocular adjustment & excellent optics, for 6 x 13cm stereo views, includes three stereo autochromes, overall excellent condition, ca. 1930s (ILLUS.) **225**

"Unis" Stereoscope

"Unis" stereoscope, by Mattey, for 6 x 13cm paper & glass views, smooth focusing & interocular adjustment mechanism, France, ca. 1920s-30s (ILLUS.) **225**

"Verascope F40" Stereoscope

"Verascope F40" transposing stereoscope, Bakelite, designed & made for F40 Stereo Camera, black, scarce (ILLUS.) **450**

"Verascope" Stereoscope

"Verascope" stereoscope, by Jules Richard, France, box-form w/reversing prism for viewing uncut stereo autotchromes or uncut stereo diapositives 45 x 107mm, includes eight uncut autochromes, viewer in excellent condition, ca. 1920, the group (ILLUS.) **600**

"Verascope" stereoscope, by Jules Richard, France, tabletop model, upright burled wood case w/ebony trim, similar to Beckers design w/chain-belt viewer but this model designed to hold 50 glass stereo slides in 45 x 107mm size, excellent optics, includes 21 slides, ca. 1915, case 8 1/2" sq., 17" h. (few rust spots on metal slide holders) **1,200**

White (H.C.) "The Perfectscope" stereo viewer, all-metal Holmes-Bates-style, the holder designed to hold a "Stereo-Pack" containing five stereo views, overall excellent condition, ca. 1911 .... **275**

Whiting's Patent Coin-op Sculptoscope

Whiting's (R.R.) Patent coin-operated "Sculptoscope," cylindrical metal case, operates by a trigger mechanism that flips the views into place, 1-cent operation, good optics, full of litho views designed for this viewer, also additional views & key, few rust spots on case, ca. 1922 (ILLUS.).. **750**

"Whiting's Patent" Sculptoscope

Whiting's (R.R.) Patent coin-operated "Sculptoscope," cylindrical metal case w/original black japanned finish w/a few rust spots, 1-cent operation, optics & mechanism in excellent condition, w/an extra box of stereo views, ca. 1922 (ILLUS.)... **800 - 1,300**

"Whiting's (R.R.) Patent" coin-operated "Sculptoscope," second model, 1-cent operation, w/lithographic stereo views, United States, ca. 1913, some rust at top of viewer, 7 1/4 x 10 1/2", 15" h. **655**

Whiting's Coin-op "Sculptoscope"

"Whiting's (R.R.) Patent" coin-operated "Sculptoscope," second model, black crinkle & glossy paint finish, 1-cent operation, the viewer full of litho stereo views specifically designed for this viewer, United States, ca. 1922, replacement top cover, glass side panels replaced by opaque perspex, coin-drop mechanism adjusted to allow for operation without coins (ILLUS.) **550**

Zeiss Tabletop Stereoscope

Zeiss stereoscope, tabletop model, w/pair of 10cm supplementary lenses in original fitted box, adjustable interocular mechanism, multiple format can be used as aid to mounting 3D slides or photographs, comes w/set of 20 glass stereo views in 3 1/2 x 7" size originally sold as optional accessory w/viewer showing technical aspects of viewer, ca. 1940s-50s (ILLUS.) **1,800**

CHAPTER 7
Stereoscope Accessories

Giveaway Boxed Set of Anaglyph Prints & Viewing Spectacles

Keystone Oak Storage Cabinet

Keystone storage cabinet, upright oak cabinet w/six top drawers w/metal drawer pulls w/nameplate slots, a long drawer at the bottom, drawers holding about 600 stereo views, bottom drawer holds a hand-held Holmes-Bates-type viewer, ca. 1900, cabinet 9 x 17", 22" h. (ILLUS.) **$726**

Set of Anaglyph prints & viewing spectacles, manufactured by the Redheffer Art Publishing Company, Chicago, Illinois, appears to be advertising giveaway for lumber/box company, w/original red/blue nose-clip spectacles & 15 Anaglyph prints, in box, rare, ca. 1900 (ILLUS. at top of page) **218**

Set of Vectograms, by the Three Dimension Co., Chicago, Illinois, includes four Vectogram transparencies & pair of Polaroid spectacles, all in original viewing box/easel, appears to have been used as some sort of eye exercise, late 1940s or 1950s (ILLUS. top of next page) **55**

"Slideoscope" Storage/Viewing Device

"Slideoscope" storage/viewing device for cabinet cards, wood w/embossed leather covering w/brass ornamentation, holds 25 double-sided frames each holding two cabinet cards, the viewed card dropping down as each new frame slides into position, w/key, patented June 21, 1892, scarce (ILLUS.) **800**

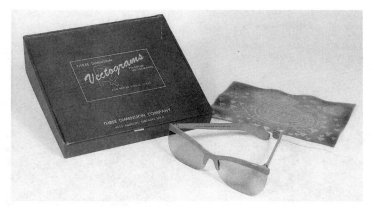

Set of Vectograms & Viewing Spectacles

Stereo Realist Store Display Viewer

Stereo Realist advertising store display viewer, designed to stimulate sales of the Stereo Realist line of cameras & viewers, large upright rectangular case w/advertising on the sides, holds 12 stereo slides, revolving mechanism & focusing work well, few light scratches on case, ca. 1950s, case 6 1/2 x 9", 10" h. (ILLUS.).. **1,400**

Lovely Mahogany Stereo View Box

Stereo view storage box, burled mahogany w/brass appliqué, rectangular w/hinged lid & rounded front, opens to two internal sections, England, ca. 1860s, 5 3/4 x 8 1/4", 5" h. (ILLUS.)............. **650**

Fancy Carved Stereo View Holder

Stereo view storage rack, walnut, ornate pierced scrolling leaf sides joined by three slanted shelves on each side, a leaf-carved handle at the top center, American-made, ca. 1870-80, overall 14" h. (ILLUS. previous page) **650**

Fancy Wooden Stereo View Rack

Stereo view storage rack, walnut, rectangular low box-form w/scroll-pierced sides & high pierced & arched center divider handle, America, ca. 1880s, excellent condition (ILLUS.) **140**

Nice Walnut Glass View Storage Box

Storage box for glass views, walnut, upright rectangular box w/flat hinged lid w/bail handle, hook latch, holds 24 glass stereo views, probably French, ca. 1870s, 4 x 7", 9" h. (ILLUS.) **275**

Storage box for stereo views, cov., papier-mâché w/grain painting & brass appliqué (ILLUS. bottom of page) **146**

Leather Storage Box for Stereo Views

Storage box for stereo views, green & purple leather w/beadwork, w/hinged slightly domed lid, "Stereoscopen" on front, Europe, probably Germany or Scandinavia, ca. 1870s, 5 1/4 x 9", 5 1/2" h. (ILLUS.) **233**

Storage box for stereo views, leather covered, w/brass plaque on top reading "Stereoscopen," the front dropping down for easy access to views, w/lock & key, 5 x 5 x 8 1/2" **700**

Papier-mâché Storage Box

Nice Mahogany Stereo View Box

Storage box for stereo views, nicely grained rectangular mahogany box, opens to two internal sections, England, ca. 1860s, excellent condition, 4 1/2 x 8 1/4", 4 3/4" h. (ILLUS.) **375**

Storage box for stereo views, rectangular black leather box w/the top of the lid embossed in gold "Stereoscopic Views," England, ca. 1860s, overall excellent condition, box 7 x 8", 5" h............................. **275**

Tabletop Storage Cabinet/Viewer

Storage cabinet/viewer for cartes de visite, walnut, tabletop model, holds up to 50 photographs on revolving belt, magnifying lens slides back & forth on two brass rods for focusing, France, ca. 1870s, 6 3/4 x 10 3/4", 10" h. closed (ILLUS.) **1,600**

Underwood & Underwood Storage Chest with Stereoscopes

Storage chest, Underwood & Underwood, w/four drawers to hold about 100 views each, the top section holding a pair of Underwood & Underwood stereoscopes, America, ca. 1900, 9 x 17", 17" h. (ILLUS.) **550**

Storage Rack for Stereo Views

Storage rack for stereo views, carved & fretwork mahogany, America, ca. 1880s (ILLUS.)... **177**

Storage rack for stereo views, walnut, America, ca. 1870s **170**

Storage rack for stereo views, walnut fret-work, America, ca. 1880, 13" h. (ILLUS.)..... **220**

Walnut Storage Rack for Stereo Views

Fine Walnut Stereo View Storage Rack

Storage rack for stereo views, walnut, rectangular open rack w/down-curved open slat sides & an arched center divided w/oblong cut-out hand hole, America, ca. 1890s, excellent condition (ILLUS.).. **650**

CHAPTER 8

Stereo Views

Stereo View of "Side Gulch"

Arizona, "Side Gulch," photographed by J. Fennimore for J.W. Powell Geological Survey, Arizona, views on the Colorado River, Glen Canyon series, #137 (ILLUS. top of page) **$120**

"Full Moon" Stereo View

Astronomy, Bierstadt View, "Full Moon," negative by Prof. Draper, image somewhat light (ILLUS.) **15**

"Moon at the First Quarter"

Astronomy, Bierstadt View, "Moon at the First Quarter," negative by Prof. Draper (ILLUS.) **30**

"Moon at the Last Quarter"

Astronomy, Bierstadt View, "Moon at the Last Quarter," negative by Prof. Draper (ILLUS.) **30**

Australia, "David's Battery, Sydney," W. Hetzer, ca. 1860, rare (ILLUS. next page, top) **350**

Aviation/balloons, "Balloon Corp - ready to ascend for observation - Lord Robert's Army advancing in Pretoria," Underwood & Underwood, from the Boer War series (ILLUS. next page, middle) **45**

Aviation/balloons, glass stereo view from balloon, France, ca. 1920s, minor emulsion flaw, 3 1/4 x 6 3/4" (ILLUS. next page, bottom) **130**

Aviation/balloons, hot air balloon in flight, glass, France, ca. 1920s, 3 1/4 x 6 3/4" (ILLUS. top of page 185) **180**

Rare Early Stereo View of Australia

"Balloon Corp" View from Boer War Series

View from Balloon

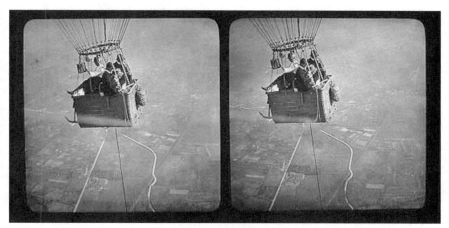

Hot Air Balloon in Flight

Stereo View of "Japanese War Balloon"

View of Copy of First Balloon Flown in America Being Inflated

Aviation/balloons, "Inflation with Hydrogen Gas of a copy of first Balloon flown in America, Jan. 9 1793, Washington Air Junction, Va.," Keystone #32338 (ILLUS.) **30**

Aviation/balloons, "Japanese War Balloon. In the rear of the besieging Port Arthur," Underwood & Underwood, from the Russo-Japanese War series 1904 (ILLUS. above, center) **45**

Aviation/balloons, "Mrs. Hoover Christens the Akron, the Largest Airship (Zeppelin) in the World, at Akron, Ohio, Aug. 8 1931," Keystone View #32766 (ILLUS. top of next page) **325**

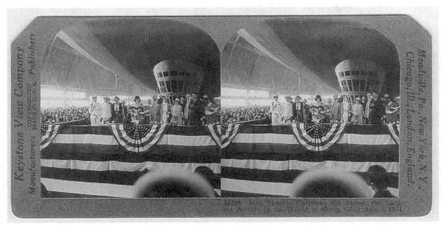

View of Mrs. Hoover Christening The Airship Akron

Two Men with Biplane

*John C. Taylor Civil War
Series #2348 Stereo View*

Stereo View of U.S. Airmail Plane

Aviation/balloons, "Professor Lowe observing the battle of Fair Oaks, Va., from his balloon," John C. Taylor Civil War series #2348 from Brady negative (ILLUS.)..... **300**

Aviation/balloons, Two men w/biplane, glass, France, ca. 1920s, 3 1/4 x 6 3/4" (ILLUS. above, center) **60**

Aviation/balloons, "United States Airmail Plane at Cleveland, Ohio," Keystone #29446 (ILLUS.).. **10**

"Baltimore Fire Engine," W.M. Chase (small spot on right image)........................... **200**

Boston view, "Summer Street," combination view, Before and After the Fire, Boston, Nov. 9 and 10, 1872, rare se-

"Summer Street" Stereo View

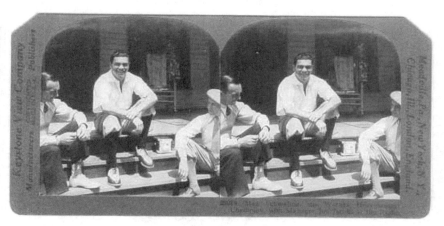

View of Boxer Max Schmeling

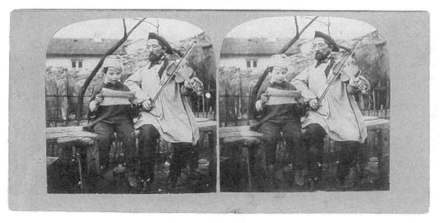

Stereo View of Boy & Fiddler

View of Lycian Saloon, British Museum

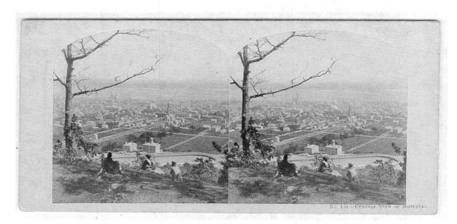

"General View of Montreal"

ries having views mounted on both sides showing scenes before and after fire (ILLUS. top of previous page) **70**

Boxing, "Max Schmeling, the World's Heavy Weight Champion. With Manager Joe Jacobs on right," Keystone, Boxing View #28028 (ILLUS. middle of previous page)... **80**

Boy & fiddler, dressed in smocks & caps, France, tiny emulsion flaw (ILLUS. bottom of previous page) **35**

British Museum, "Lycian Saloon, British Museum, Sir Charles Fellows 1841-43 at Hanthus. Frieses 500BC," by Roger Fenton, rare (ILLUS. top of page) **190**

Camera club outing, glass stereo view, excellent condition, 45 x 107mm........................ **25**

Canada, "General View of Montreal," London Stereoscopic Co., Canada series, #138 (ILLUS. above, center) **45**

Early Tinted View

Cat, early tinted view of sleeping cat on table that holds stereoscope & views, England (ILLUS.).. **25**

Charleston, South Carolina, "No. 52 Panorama from St. Michael's Church" **30**

Chicago, "Palmer House," E. Lovejoy, Chicago (ILLUS. top of next page) **30**

Chicago's "Palmer House" Stereo View

Stereo View of "Canton Joss House"

Civil War Scene at City Point, Virginia

Stereo View of "Cemetery Hill"

Civil War View of Dutch Gap Canal

Stereo View of "Evacuation of Port Royal, Va., May 30, 1864"

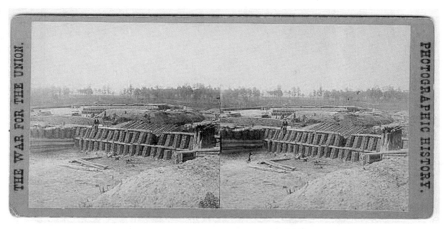

"Interior View of Fort Sedgwick" from Civil War Series

"Lulu Lake on Lookout Mountain," from Civil War Series

View of "Libby Prison, Richmond Va."

Civil War, "Interior view of Fort Sedgwick, called by the rebel soldiers 'Fort Hell', Petersburgh, Va.," E.H. & T. Anthony, neg-

ative by Brady, Civil War series, #3335 (ILLUS. top of page).................................... **180**

Civil War, "Libby Prison, Richmond Va.," E.H. & T. Anthony Civil War series #2727 (ILLUS. left).. **70**

Civil War, "Lulu Lake on Lookout Mountain," Taylor & Huntington, Civil War series, #6661 (ILLUS. above, lower) **30**

Civil War, "Rebel Soldier, killed in the Trenches of Fort Mahone, called by the Soldiers 'Fort Damnation'. This view was taken the morning after the storming of Petersburgh, Va., April 2nd, 1865," E.H. & T. Anthony, Civil War series, #3184 (ILLUS. top of next page) **300**

Civil War, "This picture is a good view of the covered ways inside the Rebel Fort

Stereo View #3184 from Civil War Series

Civil War Battle Field Scene at Fort Mahone

Wounded at Fredricksburg Civil War View

"In South Park" Stereo View

Tinted View at the Crystal Palace Exhibition

Mahone called by the soldiers Fort Damnation. The Union Soldiers had to charge up and down the obstructions. In the foreground center is a dead rebel soldier sticking out through the debris, and further on lies another Confederate soldier," E.H. & T. Anthony, No. 3183, excellent condition (ILLUS. middle of previous page) **375**

Civil War, "Wounded at Fredricksburg, Va.," by E.H. & T. Anthony, No. 2507, Brady negative, excellent condition (ILLUS. bottom of previous page) **450**

Colorado, "In South Park," from C. Weitfle's stereoscopic views of Colorado, #201 (ILLUS. top of page) **275**

Exterior View of Crystal Palace

Crystal Palace Exhibition, exterior view of Crystal Palace from Exhibition of 1855 w/statuary & fountains in foreground (ILLUS.) **70**

Crystal Palace Exhibition, tinted glass view of The Alhambra Court at the Crystal Palace Exhibition of 1855, England, excellent condition (ILLUS. above, center) **350**

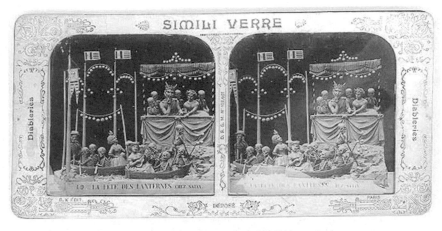

#19 Diablerie Tissue View from Simili Verre Series

"Resurrection" Diablerie Tissue View

"Un Square en Enfer" Diablerie Tissue View

Rare View of Family Using Stereoscopes

Diablerie/Devil tissue view, "Un Square en Enfer," by B.K., France, tiny tear to left image (ILLUS. top of page) **80**

Erotic view, artistically posed glass view of a semi-recumbent nude young woman posed near a window, half in sunlight, half in shadow, France, ca. 1920s, 2 x 5" **60**

Erotic view, Fine Art Publishing Company, ca. 1910, excellent condition **80**

Erotic view, glass view, France, ca. 1920s, excellent condition, 2 x 5" **70**

Erotic view, glass view of a nude young woman seated in the corner of a sofa looking right, France, ca. 1920s, 2 x 5" **250**

Erotic view, outdoor posed view of two half-nude women standing in the door-way of a stone building, from a French series by J.B., Paris, published by American Universal View Co., ca. 1900, excellent condition **65**

Erotic view, standing half-nude woman holding a large open fan atop her head,

from a French series by J.B., Paris, published by American Universal View Co., ca. 1900, excellent condition **60**

Erotic view, studio shot of a nude woman seated on a divan & peering into a mirror, from a French series by J.B., Paris, published by American Universal View Co., ca. 1900, very good condition **90**

Family portrait, unusual interior picture of an family enjoying an evening at home, four of them gathered around a table looking through stereoscopes, England, second half 19th c., some stains to mount & lower image, overall very good condition (ILLUS. above, lower) **1,200**

Florida, "The Old Cathedral, St. Augustine, Florida," J.N. Wilson, #175 (ILLUS. top of next page) **20**

Gentleman using a stereo-graphoscope, amateur view of a seated gentleman using his Rowsell Patent Stereo-Grapho-scope, sitter named on the back, late

View of "The Old Cathedral, St. Augustine, Florida"

Unusual Amateur View of a Man & His Stereo-graphoscope

19th c., excellent condition (ILLUS. above, lower) **85**

Germany, "Vue sur la port, no. 2, Hambourg," Germany, glass stereo view by Ferrier et Soulier #4207, ca. 1870 .... **275**

Hallenbach's Circus, "6428 - Group of Lions, " Keystone View, rare **150**

Ice Carnival, "Looking out of the Palace. Night view," Ice Carnival 1886/7/8, #1572, by H.H. Bennett, St. Paul, Minnesota.............. **45**

Interior of an inn or tavern, tissue hold-to-light stereo view, very strong tones & very fine quality back tinting, excellent condition, 19th c. **90**

Interior of Appleton's Stereoscopic Emporium, rare **800**

"Interior view of the Oriental Tea Co's Store, Court St. Boston, Massachusetts," W.H. Getchell **75**

View of Dresden Porcelain Exhibit at International Exhibition of 1862

King Edward VII & His Grandchildren

Portrait of King George V & Queen Mary

View of the Grecian Court at the International Exhibition of 1862

View of the International Exhibition of 1862

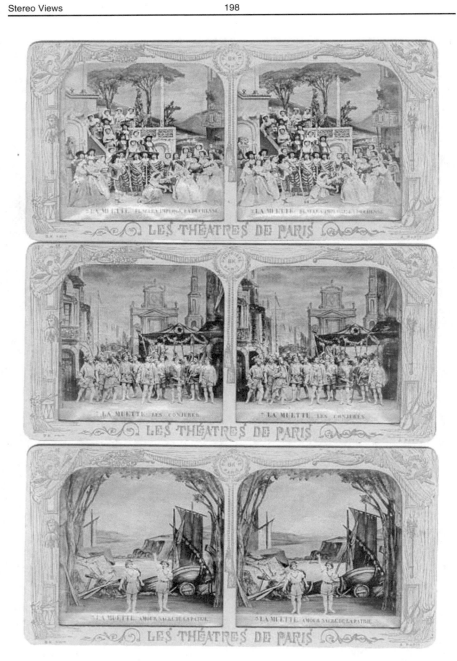

Tissue Views from Opera Set

Labor-related Stereo View

"The Tunnel in the Jackson Mine" Stereo View

*View of The North East Transept
at the International Exhibition of 1862*

King Edward VII & his grandchildren, standing in a group at Balmoral & wearing Scottish dress, Underwood & Underwood, late 19th - early 20th c., excellent condition (ILLUS. top of page) **25**

King George V & Queen Mary, standing wearing formal attire, No. 32, Underwood & Underwood, early 20th c., excellent condition (ILLUS. middle of page 197) **45**

"La Juive" opera boxed set, tissue views of various scenes from opera, complete set of 12 in original box, worn at edges, rare, the set **350**

"La Muette de Portici" opera boxed set, tissue views of various scenes from opera, complete set of 12 in original box, the interior of which lists other theatrical sets, box distressed w/some side panels missing, rare, the set (ILLUS. of 3, previous page) **400**

Labor, "Commissioners Appointed to Arbitrate the Great Coal Strike," Pennsylvania, Keystone, labor-related view #26330 (ILLUS. top of page)..................................... **70**

Lake Superior, "The Tunnel in the Jackson Mine," J. Carbutt, Views of Lake Superior, #277 (ILLUS. middle of page).................. **95**

London Bridge, tissue hold-to-light type titled "London Bridge from King William Street," transposes to a night view w/fireworks display, excellent condition w/fine back tinting, England.................................... **325**

Rare Early Stereo Lunar View - front and back

Sarony View of Mrs. Siddons

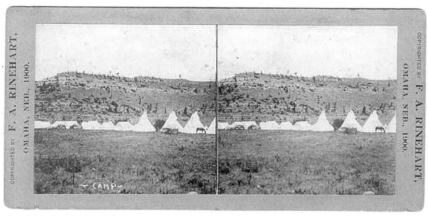

Outdoor View of a Native American Camp

"Ku-Ra-Tu and Mu Pates"

"Hepi (third son) - Wakahn-Dihiyaya"

Native American portrait, "Hepi (third son)
- Wakahn-Dihiyaya," T.W. Ingersoll, St.
Paul, Minnesota, #3208 (ILLUS.) **110**

"Kakin-Yance, Sioux"

Native American portrait, "Kakin-Yance,
Sioux," T.W. Ingersoll, St. Paul, Minneso-
ta, #3210, corner chip to mount (ILLUS.) **110**

"Ku-Ra-Tu at Rest"

Poignant Portrait of Young Native American Woman

Portrait of Wan-hesa, Sioux Lad

"Won-Si-Vu and Ku-Ra-Tu"

"The Basket Maker"

Native American portrait, "The Basket Maker," Indians of the Colorado Valley #13, photographed by Hillers for J.W. Powell Geological Survey, Arizona (ILLUS. left) **200**

Native American portrait, "Wan-hesa, Sioux Lad," No. 3207, portrait of young man standing wearing native costume & holding a small round shield in one hand, the other arm raised aloft holding weapon, T.W. Ingersoll, St. Paul, Minnesota, very good condition, late 19th - early 20th c. (ILLUS. top of page)................................. **170**

Native American portrait, "Won-Si-Vu and Ku-Ra-Tu," Indians of the Colorado Valley #28, photographed by Hillers for

Modoc War Series #1609

Native American Group Photo

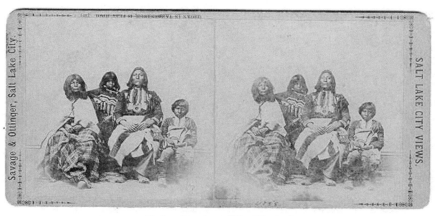

Native American "Utes" Portrait

View of Wreck near Newport, Rhode Island

Early New England View with Paddle Wheel Steamboat

View of the Brooklyn Bridge Under Construction

Unusual View of Photographer at Work above New York City

Early Ice Skating Scene in Central Park

View Showing Brooklyn Bridge Under Construction

"Broadway on a Rainy Day"

Anthony View of Fourth of July Regatta

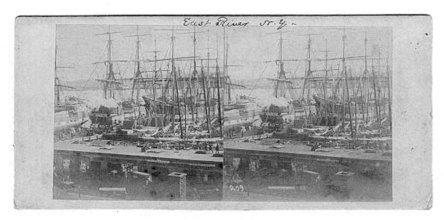

Early View of Ships Moored on the East River

Stereo View of "Union Square, West, N.Y."

Anthony View of East River (Brooklyn) Bridge

New York City, view of East River (Brooklyn) Bridge, from Anthony series "Views
of New York and Vicinity by the New
Gelatine-Bromide Process," ca. 1870s
(ILLUS.) **30**

Anthony View of Elevated Railroad

New York City, view of Elevated Railroad,
from Anthony series "Views of New York
and Vicinity by the New Gelatine-Bro-
mide Process," ca. 1870s (ILLUS.) **20**
New York City, view of the hand of the Statue of Liberty in Madison Square Park,
New York City, the hand placed there to

Early View of the Statue of Liberty Hand in New York City

"View in New York Harbor" Stereo View

help raise funds for completion of the Statue, possibly a pirated view, very slightly low contrast, ca. 1876 (ILLUS. top of page) **275**

Anthony View of Union Square

New York City, view of Union Square, East, from Anthony series "Views of New York and Vicinity by the New Gelatine-Bromide Process," ca. 1870s (ILLUS.) **30**

"No. 175 Grand Central Depot"

New York City, Views in New York and Vicinity "No. 175 Grand Central Depot," J.W. & J.S. Moulton (ILLUS.) **20**
New York Harbor, "View in New York Harbor, Steamtugs and Small Sloop under Rapid Headway," E. Anthony Instantaneous View #108 (ILLUS. middle of page) **50**

Glass View of "American Falls from Canada"

View of "On the Beach ... Lake George"

"Pallisades Mountain House"

Glass View of "Upper Fall and Railroad Bridge, Genesee"

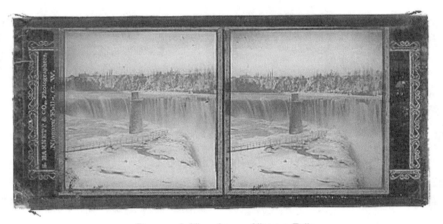

Panoramic View Across Niagara Falls

Winter View of Table Rock at Niagara Falls

View of The Niagara Falls Suspension Bridge

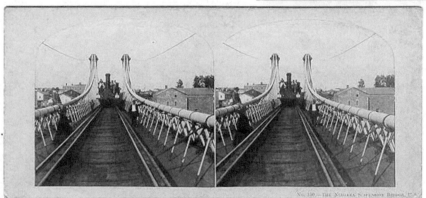

Glass View of Niagara Falls

Niagara Falls, glass view, S. Barnett & Co., ca. 1856 (ILLUS.) **120**

Niagara Falls, glass view, "Table Rock, Canada," winter view w/snow & icicles, S. Barnett & Co., ca. 1856, excellent condition (ILLUS. bottom of previous page) **325**

S. Barnett Glass View of Niagara Falls

Niagara Falls, glass view, "Table Rock from under the bank, Canada side," S. Barnett & Co., ca. 1856, rear frosted glass cracked (ILLUS.) **100**

Niagara Falls, glass view, "View under the bank looking down the River," a winter scene w/large icicles in the foreground, by S. Barnett & Co., ca. 1856, excellent condition **300**

Niagara Falls, "No. 150 - The Niagara Suspension Bridge, U.S.," from the London Stereoscopic North American Series by William England, slight soil but overall excellent condition, late 19th c. (ILLUS. top of page) **80**

"No. 94 Niagara. The Horse Shoe Fall"

Niagara Falls, "No. 94 Niagara. The Horse Shoe Fall," Anthony view (ILLUS.) **10**

"Uncle Isaac Selling Wood" Stereo View

Tissue View of Place de la Concorde

Tissue View of Paris Street

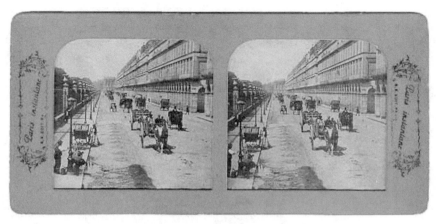

Paris Tissue View of Rue de Rivoli

Stereo View of "Elm St., Oil City, Flood of '72"

"Near Delaware Water Gap, Pennsylvania"

"Across Blue Canyon"

"Argenta Station"

Prince of Wales with Cinematographer

"Bloomer Cut near Auburn"

"Depot and Hotel at Cheyenne, Wyoming"

"Donner Lake and Pass"

"Forest View"

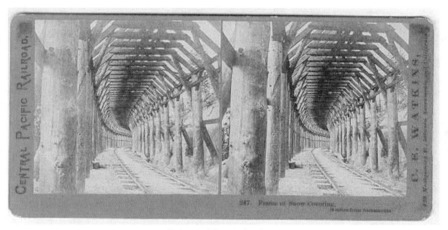

"Frame of Snow Covering"

"Giant's Gap, American River"

"Loaded Teams"

"Lower Crossing Humbolt River"

"Summit Tunnel"

Stereo View of "Pullman's Palace Train"

"Sawmill and Cut East of Cape Horn"

"Secrettown Trestle from the East"

"View on Donner Lake"

"Estes' Peak series - The Elephant"

"Cache a la Poudre series - Steamboat Rock"

"U.S. Signal Station and Observatory"

Rare Early view of Moscow

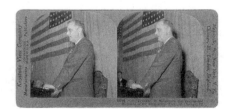

"Gov. Franklin D. Roosevelt"

"The Old San Miguel Church"

"Serenade" Tissue View

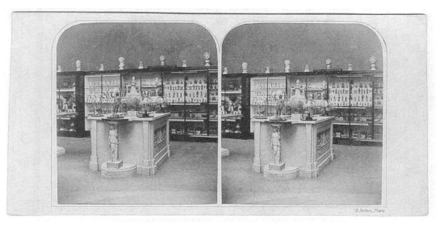

View of "Sir William Temple Collection, British Museum"

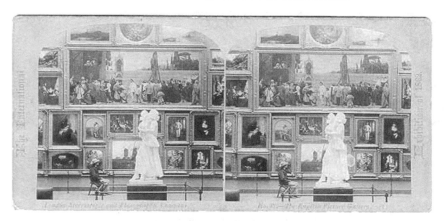

English Picture Gallery at the International Exhibition of 1862

Early Wright Aeroplane Stereo View

Portrait of General Tom Thumb Dressed as a Scotsman

General Grant and Party on the Summit of Mt. Washington

Stereo View of Salt Lake City Street

"The Fairy Wedding Party," Tom Thumb

Tom Thumb, "The Fairy Wedding Party. Mr. & Mrs. Tom Thumb, Commodore Nutt and Miss Minnie Warren," by E.H. & T. Anthony, negative by Mathew Brady (ILLUS.) **75**

Tom Thumb portrait, tinted portrait of the famous midget dressed as a Scotsman, by the London Stereoscopic Co., notation on the back "General Tom Thumb, December 28, 1858," rare, very good condition (ILLUS. top of previous page) **350**

Tom Thumb portrait, tinted view of Tom Thumb dressed in evening attire, a tiny chair & his top hat on a large table beside him, London Stereoscopic Co., somewhat speckled but overall very good condition, rare, late 1850s **325**

U.S. Grant scene, an outdoor group portrait of the large party led by General U.S. Grant on the summit of Mt. Washington, by S.F. Adams, New Bedford, Massachusetts, ca. 1870s, excellent condition (ILLUS. middle of previous page) **425**

Utah, "East Temple Street, West Side, Salt Lake City," from "Stereoscopic Gems of Utah" series, by C.W. Carter (ILLUS. bottom of previous page) **375**

Wedding views, group of 13 full-size 3 1/4 x 6 3/4" glass views, includes the bride & groom as well as many shots of the guests, excellent condition, ca. 1915-20, the group **100**

"White House, North Front, Wash. DC," from American Illustrated Series **10**

World War I glass stereo slides, 45 x 107mm glass slides together w/a focusing viewer, set of 100 in a fitted wooden box, overall excellent condition, box 7 1/2" sq., 5" h., the set **1,200**

CHAPTER 9
PHOTOGRAPHIC IMAGES
Ambrotypes

Ambrotype of African-American Man

African-American gentleman, sixth-plate size, young bearded man seated w/hands clasped & one elbow on a table, some milky tarnish on the edge, in half case, mid-19th c. (ILLUS.) **$181**

Ruby Ambrotype of Boy & Dog

Boy & dog, sixth-plate size, ruby Ambrotype of boy sitting in chair wearing suit,

embracing small dog lying on table next to him, housed in thermoplastic floral case, America (ILLUS.) **325**

Ambrotype of Boy on Bicycle

Boy on bicycle, sixth-plate size, boy wearing suit & cap sits on bike in outdoor setting, in hanging case (ILLUS.) **275**

Ambrotype of Boy with Pulltoy

Boy w/pulltoy, carte-de-visite size, little boy poses on one knee, one hand on his knee, the other holding horse pulltoy, in worn half case measuring 3 1/4 x 4 1/4", England, image measures 2 x 3" (ILLUS.) **175**
Bridal party portrait, stereo-type, by George Ruff, Brighton, England, the bride & groom seated in front w/a standing older man behind them, very sharp & well-tinted, good printed label on the

Stereo Ambrotype of a Bridal Party

back, excellent condition, ca. 1850s
(ILLUS. top of page)................................ **1,000**

Lovely Ambrotype of a Young Bride

Bride in a studio setting, three-quarter-
plate size, young woman wearing a white
wedding gown & long veil & standing behind a low balustrade, color-tinted, in an
early wide flat mahogany frame, sitter
identified, England, 1850s, image
4 x 5 1/2" (ILLUS.).. **350**

Ambrotype of British Military Officer

British military officer, oversized quarter-
plate size, a three-quarters length studio
portrait of a middle-aged officer in uniform seated facing left w/his head turned
right, slightly dark but very sharp, in full
leather case w/hinge repair, England, ca.
1855 (ILLUS.).. **400**

Two Young Girls Outdoors

Children outdoors, sixth-plate size, two young girls in dresses pose on lawn, one seated at child-size bentwood table, the other standing next to it, in hanging style half case, England (ILLUS.) **65**

Ambrotype of Young Union Soldier

Civil War image of a Union soldier, quarter-plate size ruby-type, a gaunt young man seated w/one arm resting on a table, wearing the jacket generally worn by New York State Volunteers, sharp image w/fine tones & gilt highlights on buttons, in fine thermo-plastic Union case, ca. 1861 (ILLUS.).. **400**

Union Officer in Full Dress Uniform

Civil War era officer in full dress uniform, sixth-plate size, seated wearing his elaborate uniform, holding his tall feathered hat in one hand, the other hand resting on the grip of his sword, lightly color-tinted & w/gilt highlights, excellent contrast, fine image, in full case (ILLUS.) **450**

Civil War Ambrotype of Union Soldiers

Civil War Union riflemen, quarter-plate size, ruby-type, a tall bearded man beside a shorter, younger man, each holding his rifle & bayonet upright at his side, crisp image, in half case, excellent condition (ILLUS.)... **425**

Serious Looking Young Union Soldier

Civil War Union soldier, sixth-plate size, ruby-type, a serious looking seated young soldier in uniform w/a large belt buckle & his pistol tucked into the belt, strong image w/good contrast, name of sitter written inside the case, in full but damaged Union case (ILLUS.).................... **600**

Union Soldier Wearing a Kepi

Civil War Union soldier wearing kepi, ninth-plate size, ruby-type, half-length pose of gaunt soldier wearing kepi & open coat, excellent condition, in full worn case (ILLUS.) **143**

Ambrotype of English Football Players

Ambrotype Portrait of a Bichon Frise

Dog posed sitting on a chair, sixth-plate size, by Thomas Groves, Edinburgh, Scotland, the Bichon Frise dog nicely posed sitting on a side chair, notation of photographer on back of image, very slightly dark but overall excellent condition, in full leather case, second half 19th c. (ILLUS.) **475**

English football players outside public house, quarter-plate size, rectangular, group of men standing & sitting in front of window of pub, some wearing striped jerseys & stockings, could be rugby or soccer team, housed in half hanging style case, somewhat dark around perimeter, emulsion flaw in top left corner (ILLUS. bottom of previous page) **300**

Ambrotype of English Military Officer

English military officer, half-plate size, by Antoine Claudet, three-quarters length pose facing left, in full maroon leather case w/slight warping on lid, minor spots on image, ca. 1855 (ILLUS.) **1,100**

English Military Officer

English military officer, quarter-plate size, gilt highlights, mustached man in full dress uniform sits near table, one elbow resting on tabletop, the other hand holding sword at side (ILLUS.) **250**

Exterior View of the Swan Hotel

Exterior view of the Swan Hotel, sixth-plate size, the large building w/people posed outside, sharp & clear, in hanging-style half-case frame, England, late 19th c. (ILLUS.) **225**

Gaunt Gentleman Standing with Cane

Gaunt man leaning on cane, sixth-plate size, the rather gaunt figure standing & leaning on a cane, apparently supported by a rest support whose base can be seen by his foot, excellent condition, in half case, mid-19th c. (ILLUS.)........................ **50**

Gentleman & his small dog, quarter-plate size, half-length portrait of seated serious-looking gentleman w/one hand resting on a cute little dog, re-sealed in passe-partour mount-frame, excellent condition, England, ca. 1850s **275**

Box with Inlaid Ambrotype

Gentleman inset in box, a rectangular mahogany box w/cross-banding & an inlaid diamond on the front, the top inset w/an oval portrait ambrotype of a gentleman, paper-lined interior, mid-19th c., image 1 3/4 x 2 1/4", box 7 x 10 1/2", 4 1/2" h. (ILLUS.).. **650**

Young Girl with Hoop & Stick Toy

Girl with hoop & stick, half-plate size, the standing girl wearing a large bonnet, cloak, skirt & pantalettes, holding a large hoop & stick toy, lightly color-tinted cheeks, in original case, ca. 1850s (ILLUS.) **450**

English Ambrotype of Four Fishermen

Group of men fishing, sixth-plate size, unusual outdoor scene w/four men standing by a river w/fishing poles & a net, mounted as in wall frame, excellent condition, England, mid-19th c. (ILLUS.)...................... **302**

Nice Group Portrait on a Veranda

Group of women & girls, quarter-plate size, the group of five around a table sitting on an open veranda, very sharp w/good details, in a full leather case, England, ca. 1850s (ILLUS.) **900**

Japanese Ambrotype of Three Men

Group portrait of three Japanese men, sixth-plate size, two men seated w/a standing man between them, all in traditional kimono attire, Japan, ca. 1890, in original Kiri wood case, excellent condition (ILLUS.) **400**

Ambrotype of Horse & Groom

Horse & groom outside stable, quarter-plate size, side view of standing horse w/groom, in full maroon leather case w/repaired hinge, England, ca. 1850s, excellent condition (ILLUS.) **350**

Ambrotype of Horse & Wagon

Horse & wagon, sixth-plate size, outdoor scene w/house in background, in full leather case, America (ILLUS.) **200**

Framed Ambrotype of Victorian Couple

Husband & wife, full-plate size, a middle-aged couple seated side by side in studio setting, in oval ebony shadowbox frame w/a few chips, sitters identified on the reverse, mid-19th c. (ILLUS.) **150**

Ambrotype of Male Violinist

Male violinist, large format, a three-quarters length portrait showing the man standing facing left & holding his violin & bow, his top hat on the table to his right,

in full maroon leather push-button case, re-sealed w/a gold paper mat w/a 6 x 9" opening, somewhat low contrast, couple of very minor emulsion scratches, ca. 1850s, overall 8 x 11" (ILLUS.) **650**

Man Holding Flute/Recorder

Man holding flute or recorder, in 7 1/4 x 8 1/4" composition frame w/back label reading "T. Monks Travelling Photographic Carriage," England, image measures 2 1/2 x 3" (ILLUS.) **225**

Outdoor Scene of Man on Bicycle

Man on bicycle, sixth-plate size, an outdoor view of a man seated on a safety bicycle, sharp & clear, excellent condition, housed in hanging-style half-case, England, ca. 1900 (ILLUS. bottom of previous page)... **130**

Ambrotype of Man on Horseback

Man on horseback, sixth-plate size, man wearing riding clothes sits on horse in profile against background of a brick building & wrought-iron fence, in hanging-type case (ILLUS.) **193**

Man Seated in Alleyway Setting

Man seated in alleyway setting, ninth-plate size, full-length view of a man seated in a narrow alleyway studio background, holding up & reading a newspaper in one hand, in full leather case, excellent condition, England, mid-19th c. (ILLUS.).. **300**

Studio Portrait of a Man & His Dog

Man posed with his dog, sixth-plate size, half-length portrait of a pleasant looking man seated holding his terrier under one arm, very sharp but slightly low contrast, in half leather case w/no lid, England, ca. 1850s (ILLUS.) **180**

Outdoor View of Man Beside Musket

Man seated outdoors beside musket, ninth-plate size, may be some sort of military figure since the musket is fitted w/a bayonet, England, mid-19th c., excellent condition, in full leather case (ILLUS.) **300**

Ambrotype of Man Standing in Garden

Man standing in garden with sprayer, quarter-plate size, a man standing in a garden about to spray plants w/a large wheeled contraption, he seems too well dressed to be a gardener so may be the owner or inventor of the sprayer, disturbance to the emulsion in the upper left, otherwise good contrast & sharpness, ca. 1850s (ILLUS.)..................... **200**

Nice Portrait of Matronly Woman

Matronly woman in studio pose, half-plate size, pleasant looking woman wearing a dark flounced dress, seated w/one arm

resting on a small table, plain greyish green background seems to give an almost 3D effect, very sharp, in full leather case w/hinge repair, England, ca. 1850s (ILLUS.)... **250**

Unusual View of Men in a Tea Wagon

Men in a refreshment or tea wagon, sixthplate size, outdoor scene w/two men in a covered, wheeled wagon w/ cups of tea, cakes & scones along the counter, sign in the back reads "Tea or Coffee 1d," an American flag flies from one corner of the roof to attract tourists, England, second half 19th c., excellent condition in worn hanging-style half case (ILLUS.)................. **225**

Two Men with Horse & Trap

Men w/horse & trap, sixth-plate size, two men sit in trap, one in top hat & holding whip, the other wearing derby, against background of trees, in half case missing lid (ILLUS.) **150**

Ambrotype of Man in Casual Uniform

Military man, quarter-plate size, three-quarters length portrait of a seated middle-aged man in a non-dress military uniform for either cavalry or county yeomanry, one arm resting on a table, sharp image in excellent condition, in full leather case, England, mid-19th c. (ILLUS.) **300**

Mourning Bracelet with Ambrotype

Mourning bracelet w/ambrotype, image of two women in lace caps & collars, one seated, the other standing next to her, in oval gold-plated frame, the bracelet of human hair, very unusual (ILLUS.) **588**

Niagara Falls, cased view, stamped signature on liner for Taber & Howlard, Artists, shows two men in high top hats w/three ladies standing just at the edge of the falls, leather-covered case w/burgundy velvet liner, 4 1/4 x 5 1/2" (wear to emulsion at the sides & crazing) **330**

Occupational Portrait of Butcher

Occupational portrait of butcher, sixth-plate size, man in striped apron sits gazing directly at camera, holding toddler on lap, in hanging style half case, England (ILLUS.) **200**

Ambrotype of Tool Sharpener

Occupational - tool sharpener, sixth-plate size, clean-shaven young man in shirt sleeves & dark vest w/checked tie holds tools of his trade (ILLUS.) **375**

Family Portrait Outside a Country Home

Officer of East India Company

Officer holding sword, sixth-plate size, sergeant in East India Company sitting w/one arm resting on table next to his hat, which bears the initials "EIC," the other hand holding sword that rests on his shoulder, his collar tinted red, his sergeant's stripes tinted yellow, in half case (ILLUS.) **175**

Unusual English Outdoor Ambrotype

Outdoor crowd scene, quarter-plate size, large crowd appears to be attending the laying of a foundation stone, construction area can be seen in the background w/people holding umbrellas, in full leather case w/repaired hinge, England, ca. 1850s (ILLUS.) **750**

Stereo Ambrotype of the Hagia Sophia in Constantinople

Outdoor family portrait, quarter-plate size, shows a family outside their large country home, the mother seated at the left on the porch, the little girl seated in a pony cart w/her father behind the pony & a groom standing in front of the pony, in full maroon leather case, excellent condition, England, mid-19th c. (ILLUS. top of previous page) **225**

Outdoor Scene of Harness Makers

Outdoor occupational shot of harness makers, sixth-plate size, two men wearing long work aprons standing outside their shop door, very sharp w/strong tones, excellent condition3, in a hanging-style half case, England, ca. 1850s (ILLUS.) **180**

Outdoor panorama of Constantinople, stereo-type, panorama view of the Hagia Sophia in Constantinople, Turkey, very sharp & fine quality, rare view (ILLUS. top of page) **950**

Exterior View of the Marine Hotel

Outdoor scene of a hotel, sixth-plate size, the facade of the Marine Hotel w/an English bobby in uniform standing at the right & a woman & baby standing in the doorway, very sharp but slightly dark, a couple of tiny emulsion flaws, uncased, England, second half 19th c. (ILLUS.) **130**

Outdoor scene of four children, quarter-plate size, an older boy w/three little girls all sitting on a low chicken coop, not a prosperous-looking group, very sharp w/good contrast, excellent condition, in a hanging-style half case, England, mid-19th c. (ILLUS. top of next page) **100**

Four Children Posed by a Chicken Coop

*Unusual Outdoor View
of a Sulky Horse & Driver*

*Outdoor Ambrotype
of Freight Wagon Pulled by Mules*

Outdoor scene of racing sulky horse & driver, quarter-plate size, excellent sharpness & contrast, in a full case, ca. 1850s (ILLUS.) **450**

Outdoor view of a hardware store front, sixth-plate size, a detailed image w/the store name at the top & a wide variety of the merchandise shown inside & out, clear image, scarce subject matter, in half case w/no lid, England, second half 19th c. (ILLUS. top of next page) **275**

Outdoor scene with freight wagon, sixth-plate size, a large heavily laden wagon being pulled by a team of mules, the mules tinted brown, sharp image in excellent condition, in half case, mid-19th c. (ILLUS.) **425**

Detailed Outdoor View of a Victorian Hardware Store

Unusual Outdoor View of a Store Front

Outdoor view of a store front, sixth-plate size, the image showing the full facade of the shop w/many wares on display, dealer sign at top front of building indicates he sells china, glass & earthenware, figures standing in the doorway, clear crisp image, a couple of minor emulsion breaks but overall excellent condition, England, second half 19th c. (ILLUS.) **250**

Sad Post Mortem of a Child

Post mortem of a child, ninth-plate size, half-length view w/eyes half-open, wearing a tinted red dress, mid-19th c. (ILLUS.) **75**

Unusual Ambrotype of Men Playing Cards

Group of Soldiers Dining Outdoors

Soldiers dining outdoors, sixth-plate size, the soldiers in uniform seated & standing near a long table, horses in the background, England, late 19th c., housed in hanging-style half case-frame (ILLUS.)........ **250**

Three children in a row, sixth-plate size, two young boys standing wearing tartan skirt outfits over pantaloons, a girl between them brushing the hair of the boy on the left, very sharp image, in a scarce patriotic full leather case, overall excellent condition, ca. 1850s (ILLUS. right) **1,100**

Unusual Ambrotype of Three Children

Three gentlemen playing cards, half-plate size, a horizontal image of the three men seated around a draped table playing cards, slight emulsion damage in upper right, image matted & framed, unusual subject matter, ca. 1850s, frame 8 1/2 x 10 1/2" (ILLUS., top of page)............ **950**

Ambrotype of Two Men & a Document

Two Gentlemen Shaking Hands

Two gentlemen shaking hands, quarter-plate size, full figure profile shot of two top hatted gentlemen shaking hands, in full leather case, England (ILLUS.) **275**

Two gentlemen with a document, quarter-plate size, a studio pose w/two men seated facing each other w/a document held up between them, a few spots but overall excellent condition, in full leather case, ca. 1850s (ILLUS., top of page).......... **275**

English Ambrotype of Two Girls

Two girls at table, half-plate size, young woman sits at small table that holds vase of lightly tinted flowers, while younger girl stands next to it, both dressed alike in plaid-skirted outfits, in black frame measuring 11 1/4 x 13 1/4", England, image measures 4 1/4 x 5 3/4" (ILLUS.) **225**

Two little girls, undersized half-plate size, one girl sitting on a high-backed chair & facing the standing girl to her left, each w/long sausage curls, in a half case, ca. 1850s **200**

Ambrotype Portrait of Two Men in a Friendly Pose

Early Ambrotype of Wine Drinkers

Two men drinking wine, quarter-plate size, two seated gentleman on either side of a small table holding a wine bottle & tumblers of wine, in a thermoplastic Union case, mid-19th c. (ILLUS.) **400**

Unusual Ambrotype of Men Gambling

Two men gambling, sixth-plate size, the two seated & reclining on a rug possibly playing an early version of Blackjack, very sharp image, excellent condition, in full leather case w/repaired hinge, second half 19th c. (ILLUS.) **700**

Two men in friendly pose, sixth-plate size, a studio portrait w/one man seated on the right, the other man smiling & leaning over w/his arm around the other man's shoulders, lightly color-tinted, very sharp, excellent condition, in a passe partout frame, probably English, mid-19th c. (ILLUS. top of page) **475**

English Scene of Men & Bicycles

Two men with their bicycles, sixth-plate size, two young men standing beside their safety-type bicycles, a description of the scene on the back is dated 1893, excellent condition, England (ILLUS.) **335**

Two Women with a Stereoscope

Two women with a stereoscope, quarter-plate size, studio portrait of two women wearing bonnets & jackets, seated on either side of a small table that holds a Brewster-style stereoscope, rather dark, worn velvet hanging frame, England, 1850s (ILLUS.) **110**

Two young gentlemen, quarter-plate size, relievo-type, finely tinted image of two young men in formal dress seated side by side in a studio pose, in full leather case, excellent condition, England, ca. 1850s **250**

English Ambrotype of Two Young Girls

Two young girls, quarter-plate size, color-tinted studio pose w/one girl standing beside the other seated in a chair, in a full leather case w/weak hinge, England, ca. 1850s (ILLUS.) **160**

Cased Ambrotype of Union Officer

Union Civil War officer, ninth-plate size, ruby-type, seated wearing full uniform w/one hand resting atop his drawn saber, in a thermo-plastic Union case molded w/a spread-winged eagle above the American flag & holding a banner reading "Union Forever," excellent condition (ILLUS.)............ **500**

Ruby Ambrotype of Union Officer

Union officer, quarter-plate size, ruby Ambrotype, unidentified man in full beard & wearing dress uniform stands next to American flag, in half case (ILLUS.) **600**

Unusual Photo of Woman & Her Dogs

Woman & her pet dogs, sixth-plate size, by T.C. Doane, Montreal, Canada, a studio pose of a young woman seated on the floor w/one dog on a chair beside her & the other in front of the chair, one very minor spot in upper corner, in full leather push-button case w/detached lid, unusual topic, ca. 1850s (ILLUS.)........................ **1,400**

Woman seated near a stereoscope, quarter-plate size, half-length portrait of a gaunt serious looking woman w/long curls, wearing a plaid dress, one arm resting on a table w/a Brewster-style stereoscope, image slightly dark but overall excellent condition, in full leather case, England, ca. 1850s **250**

Framed Ambrotype of Serious Woman

Woman with serious expression, half-plate size, three-quarters length color-tinted portrait of a seated middle-aged woman w/serious expression, wearing a flowered bonnet w/long ribbon ties & a dark dress, in a rectangular molded frame w/ornate scroll corners & scroll-embossed metal liner, sitter identified on the back w/an 1857 date, some wear & chips to frame (ILLUS.) **130**

Woman Standing at Desk

Woman standing at desk, half-plate size, woman w/dark full-skirted dress & dark center-parted hair stands at desk & looks out toward camera, oval matting, framed, England (ILLUS.).. **150**

Portrait of a Young Boy & Young Girl

Young boy & girl, quarter-plate size, the handsome children posed w/the boy seated on the left & the girl, probably his sister, standing & leaning on his shoulder on the right, lightly color-tinted, excellent condition, in a full case, England, ca. 1850s (ILLUS.)... **150**

Ambrotype of Young Boy & His Hoop

Young boy with his toy hoop, sixth-plate size, standing serious looking boy w/wild curly hair, holding his toy hoop in front of him, tinted blue background, sharp image, in leather flap-style case w/some edge wear & repaired hinge, ca. 1860 (ILLUS.).. **225**

Nice Ambrotype Family Portrait

Young family group, whole-plate size, a young bearded father standing to the right of his seated wife holding their baby, in full leather case, excellent condition, ca. 1850s (ILLUS.)...................... **550**

Young British Naval Apprentice

Young British Naval apprentice, over-sized half-plate size, standing w/one hand resting on piece of furniture, the other holding beribboned straw hat, wearing striped shirt & knotted scarf/tie at throat, in passe partout mount, annotation on reverse reads "Taken July 1857, John Baker Ramsey, aged 15 years. Sailed for Calcutta 25th same month," 4 1/4 x 5 3/4" image, mounted in frame 6 3/4 x 8 1/4" (ILLUS.) **2,750**

Ambrotype in Reverse-painted Case

*Stereo Ambrotype
Portrait of a Pretty
Young Woman*

Young girl in illustrated case, ninth-plate size, the pleasant looking girl w/a slight smile seated wearing a fancy lace-trimmed dress, in rare case w/cover insert reverse-painted on glass showing St. Paul's Cathedral, London, case w/repaired hinge, overall excellent condition, England, ca. 1850s (ILLUS. previous page) **750**

Young lady in a coy pose, stereo-type, partial label of English photographer, a three-quarters length portrait of a pretty young lady seated in a studio setting, her face w/a rather coy expression resting on one hand w/the arm leaning on a table, her other hand at her waist, delicately tinted flesh tones & a tinted vase on the table, very sharp w/excellent tones, ca. 1850s (ILLUS. top of page) **750**

Ambrotype of a Man and His Dog

Young man & his dog, quarter-plate size, a stern looking young man seated wearing a wide-brimmed hat, his large spotted dog curled up on a chair beside him, good contrast, excellent condition, in full case, ca. 1850s (ILLUS.) **365**

Ambrotype of Young Lady & Her Dog

Young lady seated with her small dog, sixth-plate size, very sharp image of a young lady seated facing left with her small white dog on the table beside her, in a full leather case, excellent condition, England, ca. 1850s (ILLUS.) **700**

Ambrotype of a Young Man & His Horn

Young man holding his horn, ninth-plate size, a half-length portrait of a pleasant looking young man seated holding his horn in one hand, slight low contrast but very good condition, in full case, second half 19th c. (ILLUS., previous page)............... **50**

Ambrotype of Young British Officer

Young military officer, quarter-plate size, a studio portrait of a young British military officer seated wearing his uniform & holding his pistol in his lap, his jacket & cap over-painted in red, very sharp w/good detail, housed in an ornate gilt-plaster frame, England, mid-19th c., oval image 2 3/4 x 3 3/4", frame 6 x 7" (ILLUS.) **300**

Charming Portrait of Mother & Child

Young mother & her daughter, sixth-plate size, charming pose w/a seated pretty young mother looking down at the lovely little girl on her lap, very sharp w/great tones, in full leather case, original seal w/inscription dated 1862 naming the child, overall excellent condition, England (ILLUS.).. **90**

Stereo Ambrotype of Young Woman

Young woman in profile, stereo-type, woman sitting at table holding flower in lap, very uncommon (ILLUS.) **425**

Young Woman Looking Straight Ahead

Young woman looking at camera, quarter-plate size, a three-quarters length portrait of a fairly attractive young woman seated looking directly into the camera w/her hands in her lap, fine color tinting, very sharp w/good detail, excellent condition, in full leather case, England, ca. 1850s (ILLUS.)... **170**

Portrait of a Somber Young Woman

Young woman with sad expression, sixth-plate size, seated facing right, wearing a small dark bonnet w/wide ribbon ties & a dark ruffled gown, in a full leather case w/repaired hinge, England, ca. 1850s (ILLUS.)... **95**

Woman with Stereoscope

Young woman with stereoscope, sixth-plate size, woman sitting at a table holding a Brewster-style stereoscope, in hanging-style half case w/label reading "Taken at Messrs. LaPorte & Stanley's Original Portrait Rooms, 172, King's Road, Chelsea," England (ILLUS.) **200**

Autochromes

Close-up Autochrome of Apple Blossoms

Autochrome of Autumn Landscape

Apple blossoms in close-up, a branch of apple blossoms in rich colors, marked "Fleur de Pommier - R. Dasche, Mai 1932," excellent condition, 4 x 6" (ILLUS. bottom of previous page) **225**

Autumn woodland scene, large trees in the right foreground, a path & water in the background, autumnal colors, early 20th c., excellent condition, 3 1/2 x 4 3/4" (ILLUS. top of page) **30**

Autumnal landscape, colorful fall trees in the foreground & distance, excellent condition, France, early 20th c., 3 1/2 x 4 3/4" (ILLUS.).................................... **45**

Autochrome of Beautiful Young Woman

Beautiful young woman, half-plate size, a half-length portrait of a beautiful young woman w/her hair piled high, wearing a lacy gown & long gloves & holding chrysanthemums, in an oak frame, excellent condition, early 20th c. (ILLUS.).................. **400**

Building in wooded area, stereo-type, France, 1920s, 2 1/4 x 5" (ILLUS., top next page) **30**

Tree-filled Autumn Landscape

Stereo Autochrome of French View

Stereo Autochrome of Garden

Autochrome Portrait of Officer & Lady

Autochrome Interior View of Industrial Equipment

Interior with Lady & a Spinning Wheel

Interior view of older woman at spinning wheel, unusual interior scene in a country home w/an elderly lady standing & operating a wool wheel, good color & contrast, notation on the edge reads "60 second exposure - f4.5 - lady 90 years old," slight green cast along right edge but overall excellent condition, early 20th c., image 5 x 7" (ILLUS.) **275**

Autochrome of Fashionable Lady

Lady in fashionable clothing, larger image w/lady posed wearing a long fancy cloak w/fur trim, probably a fashion publicity shot, some emulsion problems on outer edges, overall excellent condition, 1920s, 7 x 12" (ILLUS.) **550**

Autochrome of an Autumn Landscape

Landscape with autumn foliage, lovely scene in excellent condition, early 20th c. (ILLUS.) **88**

Autochrome of Cute Girl with Flowers

Little girl seated holding a basket of flowers, charming portrait, excellent condition, 3 1/2 x 4 1/4" (ILLUS.) **130**
Man in small boat at lakeside, colorful image w/the man & boat in the foreground & what appears to be a dredge in the background, rather soft focus, originated in the U.S., excellent condition, early 20th c. (ILLUS. bottom of page) **292**

Landscape with Man in a Small Boat

Autochrome of Castle Gateway

Autochrome of Two Ladies in a Garden Settings

Orchids, delicate blossoms on leafy stems, well executed & in excellent condition, early 20th c. **200**

Outdoor castle gateway scene, view of an ancient castle gateway flanked by later buildings, marked "Porte St. Marcel...," excellent condition, France, early 20th c., 4 x 6" (ILLUS.)... **90**

Outdoor garden scene with ladies, two ladies seated at a small table in a garden w/a blue flower-covered trellis behind them, probably English, excellent condition, early 20th c. (ILLUS.) **125**

Outdoor pastoral landscape with Roman aqueduct, panoramic view w/ferns in the foreground, beautiful color & contrast, excellent condition, early 20th c., 3 1/2 x 4 3/4" **75**

Stereo Autochrome of Rocamador

Lovely Sunset View of a Lake & Trees

Outdoor scene, stereo, paper label identifies scene as "Rocamador" in the Dordogne region of France, ca. 1920s, 2 1/4 x 5" (ILLUS. bottom)............................. **25**

Outdoor scene of leafy lane in autumn, shows beautiful fall colors, excellent condition, early 20th c., 5 x 7" (ILLUS. bottom of page 250).. **50**

Outdoor view of a field of irises & other flowers, very colorful, excellent condition, France, early 20th c., 3 1/2 x 4 3/4" **80**

Outdoor view of a French chateau, a landscape centered by the turreted chateau, fine color & contrast, titled "Chateau a Dadilly (?)," excellent condition, early 20th c., 4 x 6" **75**

Outdoor view of a lake at sunset, lovely panorama w/silhouetted trees in the foreground, lovely muted colors, excellent condition, early 20th c., 5 x 7" (ILLUS. top of page)... **200**

Outdoor View of a Lady in the Garden at Versailles

Stereo Autochrome of Pond

Outdoor view of a young lady in the garden at Versailles, the lady shown standing at the far right, a portion of the palace shown at the left, beautiful color & contrast, excellent condition, ca. 1920s, 5 x 7" (ILLUS. bottom prev. page) **300**

Park setting, flower beds in park-like setting, paper label marked "Autochrome Lumiere," 5 x 7" (ILLUS.) **50**

Pond w/overhanging trees, stereo-type, France, 1920s, 2 1/4 x 5" (ILLUS. top of page) **40**

"Printemps" (Spring), pastoral scene of figure & dog walking in flowering field among young trees in bud, dated 1925, 4 x 6" (ILLUS. below) **140**

Autochrome of Park Setting

"Printemps" Autochrome

French Provincial Room Interior

Room interior in French Provincial style, elegant furnishing in color, excellent condition, early 20th c., 5 x 7" (ILLUS.) **120**

Room interior in the Napoleonic style, room furnished in the style of Napoleon I w/draped walls & bed, excellent condition, early 20th c., 3 1/2 x 4 1/4" (ILLUS. below).. **85**

Room interior with French furniture, nicely lit interior showing an ornate Louis XV-style chest & Louis XVI-style armchair, minor flaw lower right otherwise excellent condition, early 20th c., 5 x 7" (ILLUS. top next page) **150**

Roses in close-up, beautiful blossoms in rich color, marked "R. Dasche, Juin 1931," excellent condition, 4 x 6" (ILLUS. bottom of next page) **80**

Napoleonic Room Interior Autochrome

Autochrome Room Interior with French Furniture

Rowing Boats on River Wye

Rowing boats on River Wye, small boats at shore of river that stretches off through wooded hills, label reads "Claude W. Parnell, Ruardean, Glos. Symonds' Yat River Wye, c. 1920," England, 4 3/4 x 6 1/2" (ILLUS.).. **75**

Close-up Autochrome of Lovely Roses

Autochrome of Alpine Logging Town

Autochrome of a Stained Glass Window

Stained glass window, vertical image of a church window w/three vertical scenes, excellent condition, early 20th c., 5 x 7" (ILLUS.).. **80**

"Ste. Foy en Tarentaise - Villaroger," scene of Alpine town showing a log pile & logging truck w/woman & two dogs perched precariously atop the logs, probably mid-1920s, 4 x 6" (ILLUS., top of page)... **75**

Sunset panorama over a French city, lovely view w/water in the foreground & buildings in the distance, labled "Autochrome Lumiere," excellent condition, France, early 20th c., 5 x 7" (ILLUS. top of next page) **90**

Three Women in a French Garden

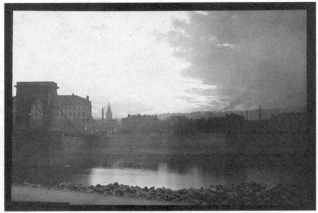

Lovely Sunset Panorama Over a French City

Three woman in a garden, an outdoor scene of three young women posed around a small flower-laden table in a French garden, beautiful color & contrast, excellent condition, early 20th c., 5 x 7" (ILLUS. bottom prev. page)............... **300**

Vase of sweet peas, studio view of a low round clear glass bowl-vase filled w/colorful sweet peas, fine contrast, excellent condition, inscribed on the edge "Pois de Senteur - Juin 1929, R. Dasche," 4 x 6" (ILLUS. below) **250**

Lovely Autochrome of a Vase of Sweet Peas

Exterior View of an Alpine Village

View of an Alpine village, a view of water & rustic buildings on the outskirts of the town, titled "Les Breviers - Alt. 1572 m," excellent condition, France, early 20th c., 4 x 6" (ILLUS.)... **75**

Well-lit Portrait of a Woman & Flowers

Woman in a well-lit interior pose, a half-length pose of a middle-aged woman seated w/flowers in front of her & light shining in from the right, excellent condition, France, early 20th c., oval mat 3 1/2 x 4 1/2", overall 5 x 7" (ILLUS.) **160**

Autochrome of Woman with Parasol

Woman seated holding parasol, imposing looking woman wearing Chinese-style dress & holding a large parasol, very colorful, only a small imperfection around the lip area, early 20th c. (ILLUS.) **83**

Woman seated in a wicker armchair, an interior view w/sunlight pouring in a window in the background, housed in a deluxe Diascope case, both in excellent condition, image 3 1/2 x 5", the set (ILLUS. of both, top next page).................... **325**

Autochrome of Woman in Wicker Chair & the Diascope Case Holding It

Stereo Autochrome of Woods

Young woman in long gown, the slender young woman w/her dark hair pulled back standing in a studio setting & wearing a long fancy kimono-style gown, housed in a Diascope viewing frame, ca. 1930, 5 x 7" **300**

Autochrome of Woodland Path

Woodland path, gnarled tree trunk in foreground against background of path winding through wooded setting, France, 1930s, 3 1/2 x 4 3/4" (ILLUS.) **20**
Woods, stereo-type, image of path winding through trees, France, 1920s, 2 1/4 x 5" (ILLUS., middle next column) **30**

Autochrome of Pretty Young Woman

Young woman standing by garden gate, wearing a loose flowered jacket & long pleated skirt, probably taken w/a panoramic camera turned vertically, rich col-

or, excellent condition, pre-1920, 3 1/2 x 7" (ILLUS. prev. page)...................... **200**

Cabinet Cards

Figures Posed with Camera

Boy & young woman with camera, the young woman seated w/what appears to be a London Stereoscopic Company "Artist's Hand Camera" on lap, the boy standing w/hand on camera, on card reading "Lambert Lilley - Boscombe - Bournemouth" (ILLUS.)............................... **150**

Cabinet Card of Mounted Cavalry Officer

Cavalry officer on horse, by Henry Linn of Woolwich, cavalryman in uniform sits atop horse in front of ivy-covered building (ILLUS.)... **20**

Portrait of Edward, Prince of Wales

Edward, Prince of Wales, by W.D. Downey, shown as a youth while a student at Eton, he later became King Edward VIII who abdicated to marry Wallis Simpson, mount w/some edge wear & slight delamination, overall excellent condition (ILLUS.)... **80**

Cleverly Posed Group of Young Women

Group of young women, by C.L. Walker, Grinnell, Iowa, cleverly posed group of young women posed as artists & works of art, slight soil to mount, overall excellent condition, ca. 1890 (ILLUS.) **200**

Lady Brooke, Countess of Warwick

Lady Brooke, Countess of Warwick, by Wallery, beautiful young woman rumored to be one of the mistresses of King Edward VII, posed in a widely draped formal gown, seated w/head turned to the left, excellent condition (ILLUS.) **45**

Portrait of Lady in Studio Setting

Lady standing in studio setting, by Hotchkiss of Norwich, New York, the rather rotund lady standing wearing a draped gown, one hand on a table holding a pedestal stereoscope, very slight edge wear to mount, very good condition, ca. 1880s (ILLUS.) **45**

Cute Little Girl & Her Teddy Bear

Little girl & her Teddy bear, charming studio portrait of a toddler standing next to a low table & holding the arms of her Teddy bear, slight damage in corner of thin tan mount, strong sepia tones, overall excellent condition, early 20th c. (ILLUS.) **100**

Little Girl with Camera on Tripod

Outdoor Group Portrait of Mixed Musical Ensemble

Little girl with camera on tripod, smiling fair-haired girl w/long curls & big bow in hair stands next to camera as though directing a pose, marked "Atelier Schubert Bad Wildungen," Germany, ca. 1900 (ILLUS., bottom prev. page)........................ **170**

Musical ensemble portrait, albumen print of a large group of male & female musicians posed standing, seated or reclining outside, rich sepia tones, excellent condition, ca. 1900, matted, image 7 x 10" (ILLUS., top of page)........................ **45**

Older couple posed with Becker-style stereoscope, man in suit w/cane stands next to stout seated woman whose arm rests on table holding stereoscope, mounted over another image (ILLUS.)........... **55**

Masonic Portrait of Jabez Hogg

Portrait of Jabez Hogg in Masonic regalia, by Mayall, Hogg being the author of a

Couple with Stereoscope

sought-after book, "The Microscope: Its history, construction and application," published in 1854, and early photographer, the card inscribed & autographed by him, small split or puncture to the right of his face, England, late 19th c. (ILLUS.) **75**

Post mortem photo of an older gentleman, posed lying on a bed dressed in his best suit & gloves, excellent condition **35**

Post Mortem Portrait Cabinet Card

Post mortem portrait, man in a casket wearing fez (ILLUS.) **40**

Prince Albert Victor, Son of Edward VII

Prince Albert Victor, Duke of Clarence & Avondale, by W. & D. Downey, the prince dressed in a fancy military uniform, he was the eldest son of King Edward VII & died in 1892, excellent condition (ILLUS.) **95**

Princess Mary of Teck, later to become Queen Mary, wife of King George V of England, by Gunn & Stewart (ILLUS., top of column) **35**

Cabinet Card of Princess Mary of Teck

Queen Victoria in donkey cart, outdoor view including her servant John Brown at the right, by Gunn & Stewart, slight soil to mount & image slightly light, rare view **110**

Portrait of Queen Victoria in 1897

Queen Victoria seated at a table, by Gunn & Stewart, taken in the 60th year of her reign in 1897, shows her seated facing left, leaning one elbow on a table & apparently looking at a stereo Daguerreotype, possibly of her late husband, Prince Albert, mount w/some light soil, overall excellent condition (ILLUS.) **90**

Cabinet Card of Theatrical/Magician Types

Two theatrical/magician types, by Scott & Wilkinson, Cambridge, the man on left holding & pointing to a padlock, the one on right holding & appearing to consult a pocket watch (ILLUS.) **25**

Two young men with their new bicycles, unknown photographer, late 19th c., excellent condition **30**

Victorian Couple with Stereoscope

Woman & gentleman in studio setting, seated woman appears to hold a Holmes-Bates-style stereoscope, views & an album on the table between them, by Mudge & Mudge, Elkhart, Indiana, ca. 1890s, slight soil on mount (ILLUS.) **35**

Framed Cabinet Card of Woman

Woman beside table, woman standing next to table upon which are a stereoscope & photographs, mount trimmed at bottom, in late Victorian frame measuring 12 1/4 x 14 1/4" (ILLUS.) **110**

Young Kansas Lady & Her Bicycle

Young woman with her safety bicycle, by Hartin of Hutchinson, Kansas, a young lady standing behind her new safety bicycle in a studio setting, excellent condition, ca. 1890s (ILLUS.) **35**

Cartes de Visite

Portrait of Opera Star Adelina Patti

Adelina Patti, opera star, by The London Stereoscopic & Photographic Company, Patti (1834-1919) was a celebrated Victorian opera singer, half-length image shows her costumed as Juliet, ca. 1870s, excellent condition (ILLUS.) **35**

Anthony Trollope, English author, by The London Stereoscopic & Photographic Company, scarce (ILLUS.) **40**

Portrait of Prime Minister Disraeli

Benjamin Disraeli, British Prime Minister, by W. & D. Downey, half-length portrait of the seated Disraeli facing left, second half 19th c., excellent condition (ILLUS.) **35**

CDV of Anthony Trollope

CDV of Captain Matthew Webb

Early Carte View of the Quebec, Canada Waterfront

Captain Matthew Webb, first man to swim English Channel, by Fredelle & Marshall, unknown whether autograph below image is actual signature or facsimile (ILLUS., bottom prev. page) **25**

City of Quebec docks, by L.P. Vallee, outdoor panorama looking down on the docks & busy riverfront, a few spots on the mount, otherwise excellent condition w/strong tones (ILLUS., top of page) **20**

CDV of Charles Darwin

Charles Darwin, English scientist, by Berraud & Jerrard, rare, somewhat grainy (ILLUS.) **45**

CDV of Young Union Officer

Civil War officer portrait, by Fredericks of New York City, young officer in full dress uniform standing in a studio setting, excellent condition, ca. 1860s (ILLUS.) **150**

CDV of Edwin Landseer R.A.

CDV of Henry Wadsworth Longfellow

CDV of Empress Eugenie

Images from Group of Cartes de Visite Featuring Egyptian Scenes

Images of Egypt, group of shots of Egyptian life/culture, the majority of people of various occupations & backgrounds, some geographical scenes, five w/photographer's imprint (Meissner, Bonfils, Hammerschmidt, two Beato), condition varies from good to excellent, ca. 1860s-70s, group of 30 (ILLUS. of 10) **600**

Lord Palmerston, Prime Minister to Queen Victoria, by Camille Silvy, excellent condition (ILLUS.) **65**

Occupational CDV of Butcher's Apprentice

Occupational - butcher's apprentice, by J. Monte, Camden Town, London (ILLUS.) **15**

Carte de Visite of Lord Palmerston

CDV of Otto Edward Leopold Von Bismark

Otto Edward Leopold Von Bismark, by Loescher & Petsch of Berlin, image of German statesman in military uniform sitting in chair (ILLUS.) **20**

Carte View of the Market in Algiers

Outdoor market in Algiers, by Clavier, second half 19th c., excellent condition (ILLUS.).. **35**

Pair of Nautical CDVs

Pair of nautical scenes, the smaller (2 1/2 x 4") image, by W.H. Mitchell, showing a sailor from the Royal Navy ship HMS St. Vincent, the larger (3 1/4 x 4 3/4") image, by G.W. Wilson, of the ship itself, pr. (ILLUS.) **30**

Unusual Carte of a Photographer

Photographer at work, man standing behind his plate camera on a tripod, dated 1885 on the back, slightly low contrast but overall excellent condition (ILLUS.)
.... **250**

prince in later life, fine tonal quality, excellent condition (ILLUS.) **130**

Unusual Advertising Carte-de-Visite

Photographic advertising carte-de-visite, from Sarony, image shows a flood of cartes pouring out of crossed cornucopias at the top, the reverse w/advertising & promotional quotes, ca. 1863, excellent condition (ILLUS.) **160**

Prime Minister W.E. Gladstone, by Elliot & Fry, England, ca. 1860s, excellent condition **30**

CDV of Prince & Princess Louis of Hesse with Their Children

Prince & Princess Louis of Hesse w/children, by Hills & Saunders, slightly soiled (ILLUS.).. **20**

Carte Image of Princess Mary Adelaide

Princess Mary Adelaide, Duchess of Teck, by Camille Silvy, ca. 1860s, excellent condition (ILLUS.) **45**

Formal Portrait of Prince Albert

Prince Albert, Consort of Queen Victoria, by Camille Silvy, standing portrait of the

CDV of William Thomson Kelvin

William Thomson Kelvin, English mathematician/physicist, by Thomas Annan of Glasgow, rare (ILLUS.) **45**

Young Girl Holding Brewster Stereoscope

Young girl holding Brewster stereoscope, by J. Petersens, Jönköping (ILLUS.).. **35**

Daguerreotypes

American Family Portrait

American family portrait, quarter-plate size, very serious mother & father seated flanking their standing little girl w/her long sausage curls & holding a small bouquet of flowers, her dress tinted light blue & the flowers also tinted, re-sealed in case, minor edge tarnish, ca. 1850s (ILLUS.)
.... **332**

Young American Mother & Her Child

American mother with her toddler, sixth-plate size, the pretty dark-haired young mother seated holding her curly-haired toddler who moved slightly during the shot, some edge tarnish, re-sealed in full case, ca. 1850s (ILLUS.) **88**

Statuary Garden at the Crystal Palace Exhibition

American Navel Officer Daguerreotype

Cute Chubby Girl Seated in a Big Chair

American Naval Officer or Midshipman in uniform, half-plate size, three-quarters portrait wearing uniform w/gold-trimmed buttons, excellent tones & sharpness, re-sealed in full leather case (ILLUS.) **1,300**

Chubby little girl seated in a chair, sixth-plate size, the little miss w/neatly combed curls sits w/her hands in her lap, wearing a lightly red-tinted dress, cheeks lightly tinted cheeks, minor edge tarnish, re-sealed in full case, ca. 1850s (ILLUS.)......... **210**

Crystal Palace Exhibition view, stereo-type, a picture of the statuary garden at the exhibition in 1855, attributed to Phil-lipe Delamott or his operator, T.R. Will-iams, a couple of very minor spots but overall excellent condition, cased w/the original seal (ILLUS., top of page)............... **900**

Daguerreian Pin or Brooch

Daguerreian pin or brooch, sixth-plate size, head shot of unsmiling young man gazing off to side, in ornate oval frame in full leather case, America (ILLUS., bottom previous page) **750**

Dual Portrait of Children

Dual portrait of children, quarter-plate size, two toddlers who appear to be twins sitting on couch, the one on the left sitting upright & gazing into camera, the one on the right w/bare feet lying on side w/eyes closed, probably post mortem, original seal in full case (ILLUS.) **3,300**

English Family Group

English family group, quarter-plate size, fair-haired boy stands between woman w/sausage curls & man in high collar holding book, unusual horizontal format, re-sealed in full push-button case (ILLUS.).. **420**

Daguerreian English Family Portrait

English family portrait, quarter-plate size, the middle-aged parents seated in front of their standing teenage daughter, some edge tarnish, original seal in full case, England, ca. 1850s (ILLUS.)........................ **200**

Untinted Portrait of English Gentleman

English gentleman, quarter-plate size, by Beard's Photographic Institution, re-sealed in full Beard case (ILLUS.) **165**

Family group, half-plate size, man & woman sitting surrounded by girls & boys of various ages, full case **500**

Family Group Daguerreotype

Family group, quarter-plate size, woman sits in the midst of five children of various ages, the smallest girl clutching a doll, resealed in full case (ILLUS.) **400**

Rare Australian Family Portrait

Family group portrait, quarter-plate size, by Kopisch & May of Adelaide, Australia, a studio portrait of a mother & father flanking their young daughter, his arm around the girl's shoulders, delicately tinted, fine condition in full leather case w/original seal & paper label for the photographer, rare image (ILLUS.) **850**

Family portrait, half-plate size, an older gentleman seated across from his younger-looking wife on a long sofa w/a teenage boy leaning over the back in the center, ribbon on woman tinted pink, resealed, very minor plate imperfections, mid-19th c. (ILLUS., bottom of page) **800**

Nice Daguerreian Family Portrait

American Daguerreotype Family Portrait

Family portrait, quarter-plate size, a middle-aged couple seated w/their young son standing between them, very sharp image, re-sealed in a geometric Union case, excellent condition, America, ca. 1850s (ILLUS.) **325**

Rare Early Portrait of a Fireman

Family Portrait

Family portrait, sixth-plate size, man sitting surrounded by three girls of various ages, original seal in full case (ILLUS.).................. **325**

Fireman in dress uniform, sixth-plate size, the standing young man wearing a top hat & fancy cap, the large metal buckle on his belt reads "Hope Hose Co.," he holds a fire horn in one hand, probably from the Philadelphia area, some edge tarnish & a stain at the top, original seals in a half case, ca. 1850 (ILLUS.)............... **1,400**

Daguerreotype of Freemason

Freemason, sixth-plate size, man wearing sash holds book, the sash tinted red, uncommon, re-sealed in full but damaged Union case (ILLUS.)..................................... **300**

French military officer, quarter-plate size, by Derussy, officer w/mustache & goatee wearing kepi & uniform featuring fringed epaulettes & medal on breast sits framed in draped background, France, ca. 1845 .... **875**

Portrait of Man with a Stamped Letter

Gentleman holding a letter, sixth-plate slightly undersized size, shown half-length seated facing right, lightly tinted including the stamp on the letter that is tinted orange to represent the two-penny red stamp of the mid-1840s, in case w/original seal, some edge tarnish, England (ILLUS.).. **150**

Half- plate Daguerreotype of a Man

Gentleman, half-plate size, image of older man in suit & vest, by McClees & Germon, resealed in full leather case (ILLUS.).. **325**

Gentleman in Possible Naval Uniform

Gentleman in close-up portrait, quarter-plate size, half-length view of balding gentleman who appears to be wearing a Naval uniform, very sharp image w/great tones & contrast, re-sealed in half leather case missing lid, America, ca. 1850s, excellent condition (ILLUS.)............................. **450**

Gentleman Resting Arm on Chairback

Portrait of Gentleman by Mayall

Gentleman leaning on a table, quarter-plate size, by Jeremiah Gurney, the man seated facing right w/one arm resting on the crest of his chair, his stove pipe hat on the table beside him, tinted flesh tones & light blue cloth on table, very sharp w/excellent tones, re-sealed in full leather case w/repaired hinge, New York, New York, ca. 1850s (ILLUS.)................................ **350**

Gentleman seated facing right, ninth-plate size, gentleman in suit & wearing spectacles, color-tinted, re-sealed in early top-hinged maroon leather case, England, ca. 1850s, excellent condition **150**

Gentleman seated in armchair, quarter-plate size, by Mayall, color-tinted half-length portrait of a balding gentleman seated facing left, a couple of very slight mat abrasions, re-sealed in full maroon leather case w/Mayall logo embossed on obverse, ca. 1850s (ILLUS.) **425**

Gentleman seated in studio setting, ste-reo-type, finely color-tinted & posed half-length portrait of a middle-aged gentle-man seated facing right w/one arm rest-ing on a table, by Antoine Claudet, origi-nal seal, in slipcase w/Claudet & royal coat-of-arms, case w/a tear but overall excellent condition, ca. 1855 (ILLUS.) **1,800**

Stereo Daguerreotype of a Gentleman in a Studio Setting

Daguerreotype of Gentleman with Spectacles

Gentleman wearing spectacles, stereotype, by J.H. Whitehurst, Baltimore, re-
sealed & housed in quarter-plate leather push-button Mascher stereoscopic viewing case (ILLUS.) **950**

Gentleman wearing spectacles, stereotype, some edge tarnish & a tiny plate flaw, re-sealed in quarter-plate leather push-button Mascher viewing case, America, ca. 1853 (ILLUS., bottom of page) **900**

Daguerreian Portrait of a Gentleman

Gentleman with curly hair, quarter-plate size, by Gurney, half-length portrait of a distinguished looking middle-aged gentleman w/curly dark hair, very sharp, excellent condition, re-sealed in full leather push-button case, New York, New York, mid-19th c. (ILLUS.) **400**

Stereo Daguerreotype of a Gentleman Wearing Spectacles

Handsome Young Couple & Infant

Group portrait of a young family, sixth-plate size, the handsome young couple seated holding their new infant between them, the father w/his hand on the baby's head to prevent movement, the mother w/a smiling expression, very lightly color-tinted, some insignificant edge tarnish,

re-sealed in full leather case, England, ca. 1850s (ILLUS.)........................ **550**

Daguerreotype of Three Siblings

Group portrait of three siblings, sixth-plate size, the three children arranged in a row w/the older girl on the left & her brother at her right w/his arm around the toddler beside him, excellent condition, re-sealed in half leather case w/no lid, ca. 1850s (ILLUS.)... **200**

Group portrait of two couples, quarter-plate size, a young man at each end w/two young women seated between them, minor edge tarnish, in full case w/partial original seal, ca. 1850s (ILLUS., bottom of page)... **175**

Group Portrait of Two Young Couples

Italian Court at Crystal Palace, London

Group Portrait of a Musical Trio

Group shot of a musical trio, quarter-plate size, by Bogardus, three young men seated in a row, perhaps a vocal trio, the central figure holding an accordion, some edge tarnish, re-sealed in marked full case, New York, New York, ca. 1850s (ILLUS.)... **1,000**

Italian Court at Crystal Palace, London, stereo-type, large shell in foreground, w/classical figures & columns in background, label on obverse indicates the image was sold by H. Negretti & Zambra, official "Photographers to the Crystal Palace Company," ca. 1855, some minor tarnish at top of image (ILLUS., top of page).. **800**

Daguerreian Portrait in a Brooch

Lady in brooch necklace, small oval image w/a half-length portrait of a stern looking woman seated facing left & wearing an off-the-shoulder dress, in a stamped gold mount w/ring suspended from a chain, excellent condition, ca. 1850s, image 1 x 1 1/4" (ILLUS.).. **350**

Daguerreotype of a Victorian Lady Taken by Baker in India

Lady in ruffled dress, stereo-type, by F.W. Baker, Calcutta, India, half-length portrait of a serious looking woman seated wearing a fringe-trimmed jacket over a ruffled dress, one arm resting on a table, in a Claudet-style folding viewing case, a few small rust-colored spots on the image, image very lightly tinted & very sharp, case also in excellent condition & marked w/the Baker logo, image re-sealed w/part of the original seal intact, ca. 1850s (ILLUS.).. **3,000**

Lady seated by small table, sixth-plate size, a full-length portrait of a lady seated w/one arm resting on a small table, very sharp, re-sealed in a full maroon leather case, excellent condition, England, ca. 1850s (ILLUS., right) **120**

Daguerreian Portrait of a Victorian Lady

Attractive Woman Wearing Headband

Lady wearing unusual headband, ninth-plate size, a half-length studio pose of an attractive woman standing facing left, a decorative band across her parted hair, lightly tinted flesh tones & a light blue dress, original seal, in early top-hinged full leather case, England, ca. 1850s (ILLUS.).. **200**

Charming Portrait of Boy & Girl

Little boy & little girl, sixth-plate size, charming portrait of young brother & sister posed in a large chair, original seal, in full leather case, excellent condition, ca. 1850s (ILLUS.)... **325**

Little Boy Posed in a Fancy Suit

Little boy dressed in Lord Fauntleroy-style outfit, sixth-plate size, posed seated on the edge of a draped table w/one hand on the back of a balloon-back side chair, very sharp, wide tarnish ring around edges, overall excellent condition, in half leather case, ca. 1850s (ILLUS.)... **150**

Daguerreotype of Little Girl

Little girl, sixth-plate size, little girl sits sideways on chair, one hand holding back of chair, her feet resting on chair rung, re-sealed in half case (ILLUS.)..................... **110**

Little girl clutching a small doll, ninth-plate size, by Beard, the cute toddler seated w/her hair parted in the center & pulled back, holding a small doll in her lap, her mother's hand seen to the left side, delicately color-tinted, re-sealed in an early top-hinged leather case

Portrait of Cute Little Girl with a Doll
w/Beard's handwritten signature on the case, slightly soft focus but excellent condition, England, ca. 1850s (ILLUS.) **225**

Tinted Portrait of a Little Girl

Very Young Girl Holding Her Doll

Little girl & her doll, ninth-plate size, cute oval portrait of a young toddler clutching her china-head doll, original seal, in an oval case w/maroon velvet covering, some edge tarnish, overall excellent condition, England, ca. 1850s (ILLUS.) **300**

Little girl seated by table, sixth-plate size, nicely color-tinted studio portrait of a young girl seated atop a side chair beside a cloth-covered table, original seal, in half leather case missing the lid, England, ca. 1850s, excellent condition (ILLUS., top next column) **300**

French Portrait of Girl in a Small Chair

Little girl seated in a small chair, sixth-plate size, by Belloc, oval portrait of a very serious looking young girl seated in a small ladder-back chair, holding a bouquet of flowers & a closed parasol across her lap, flowers & parasol finely color-tinted, in a passe-partout frame w/original seal, France, ca. 1850s **900**

Little girl standing beside a chair, sixth-plate size, charming child wearing a ruffled dress & pantaloons, original convex glass & seal in excellent condition, in full leather case, America, ca. 1850s **500**

Daguerreotype of Pretty Young Girl

Little girl standing beside a table w/a basket of flowers, half-plate size, finely color-tinted image, re-sealed in full maroon leather push-button case, unknown photographer, England, ca. 1850s (ILLUS.).. **650**

Girl in Tinted Dress Standing by a Chair

Little girl standing beside a tall-backed chair, sixth-plate size, by Broadbent, the pretty but solemn girl standing wearing a long checked light blue-tinted dress, one hand holding a spindle in the chair back, some edge tarnish, re-sealed in full case, Philadelphia, Pennsylvania, ca. 1850s (ILLUS.).. **484**

Man seated with Colt-type pistol in his belt, sixth-plate size, image w/large wipe on left side & a couple of minor mat abrasions, re-sealed & housed in full-leather case, America, ca. 1850s **400**

Sixth-plate Daguerreotype of Couple

Man & woman, sixth-plate size, "Photographic Portrait Gallery ... Arcade, Manchester" embossed on front of full leather case, England (ILLUS.).................... **180**

Man & woman posed in studio, stereotype, tinted, the woman in elaborate dress sitting next to man in suit in studio setting of parlor decorated w/Victorian-style wallpaper & drapes, by Antoine Claudet, the Claudet label on obverse identifying the studio at "107, Regent Street, London," housed in Claudet slip-case, image re-sealed (ILLUS., below) **2,500**

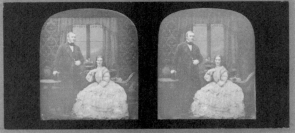

Tinted Stereo Daguerreotype by Antoine Claudet

Rare Stereo Daguerreotype of a Nude

Cooley Portrait of a Mother & Daughter

Mother & daughter, half-plate size, the daughter wearing an off-the-shoulder dress standing at the right w/her arm on the shoulder of her mother seated at the left, by Cooley of Springfield, Massachusetts, great tonal gradation & sharp detail, re-sealed in full case, excellent condition, ca. 1850s (ILLUS.)...................... **900**

Daguerreotype of Mother & Daughters

Mother & daughters, half-plate size, a stocky woman flanked by her two young daughters, sharp image w/good contrast, very minor spots on plate, overall excellent condition, re-sealed in half leather case, America, mid-19th c. (ILLUS.) **850**

Mother & sons, quarter-plate size, charming portrait w/light color tinting, re-sealed in case, some edge tarnish, mid-19th c. **250**

Nude seated with a guitar, stereo-type, artistic image w/fine color tinting, prefect condition, France, mid-19th c., re-sealed (ILLUS., top of page)................................. **6,500**

Stereo Daguerreotype of Nude Statuary

Nude statuary, stereo-type, by Pradier, classical female figure in diaphanous robes lounges on oval base, sold by M.S. Marchi, France (ILLUS., bottom prev. page) **532**

Occupational Portrait of Artisan

Occupational - artisan, sixth-plate size, man wearing apron & w/sleeves rolled up holds hammer in one hand & chisel in the other, full leather case & original seal (ILLUS.) **1,060**

Portrait of Choirmaster

Occupational - choirmaster, quarter-plate size, bearded man in suit holding what appears to be tuning fork in one hand & sheet music in other, re-sealed in half case (ILLUS.) **400**

Older couple, quarter-plate size, woman wearing bonnet & shawl sitting w/man

holding walking stick, by John Plumbe Jr., re-sealed in full "Plumbe" case & mat, paper label underneath image reads "Manufactured at the Plumbe National Daguerrian Depot, New-York" **850**

Fine Portrait Daguerreotype by Beard

Older gentleman, by Beard, quarter-plate size, half-length portrait of the seated older gentleman facing left, fine quality color tinting, re-sealed in full maroon leather case w/Beard coat-of-arms in gilt, excellent condition, England (ILLUS.) **350**

Langenheim Portrait of Older Woman

Older woman, sixth-plate size, by Langenheim Bros., Philadelphia, a half-length portrait of a stout older woman seated facing left & wearing a lacy cap, some edge tarnish, re-sealed in full case (ILLUS.) **500**

Fine Outdoor Daguerreotype Showing a House and People

Outdoor landscape with a house, quarter-plate size, a two-story house w/trees in the front yard behind a white rail fence, a man & boy posed by the fence, very sharp w/fine tonal values, minor stain in bottom center left, re-sealed in full case, mid-19th c. (ILLUS., top of page)............. **2,500**

Daguerreian Portrait of an Older Woman

Older woman in seated pose, ninth-plate size, full-length studio portrait of a seated older woman wearing a lacy cap & collar & long-sleeved full dress, re-sealed in early top-hinged maroon leather case, image & case in excellent condition, England, ca. 1850 (ILLUS.)........................ **170**

Rare Outdoor Daguerreotype View

Outdoor scene of house & country road, oversized quarter-plate size, probably in New England, some edge tarnish but overall excellent condition, re-sealed in full leather case, case 4 1/4 x 4 3/4" (ILLUS.)... **2,000**

Daguerreian Portrait of a Pensive Woman

Pensive woman wearing a shawl, sixth-plate size, the half-length studio portrait of a woman seated facing left holding her hands in her lap, excellent tones & sharpness, flawless condition, re-sealed in full leather case, England, ca. 1850s (ILLUS.).. **300**

Daguerreotype of a Portrait Drawing

Portrait drawing of a gentleman, quarter-plate size, by Kilburn, shows a well done bust portrait of a middle-aged gentleman, re-sealed in full Kilburn case, England, ca. 1850s (ILLUS.) **333**

Portrait of English Midshipman, sixth-plate size, by Helsby of Valparaiso, Chile, half-length portrait w/sitter looking left, re-sealed in full leather push-button case, few minor rust spots but overall excellent, paper label on back names sitter & is dated 1854, Helsby was English by birth but ran his studio in Chile for many years, ca. 1850s **1,100**

Sixth-plate Daguerreotype of Gentleman

Portrait of gentleman, sixth-plate size, re-sealed & housed in full maroon top-hinged leather case, England (ILLUS.) **130**

Man in Light-colored Suit

Portrait of man, quarter-plate size, man sporting side whiskers & wearing light-colored suit & hat tilted at somewhat rakish angle smiles slightly at camera, lips & cheeks tinted, in full case (ILLUS.) **325**

Gurney Portraits of a Husband & Wife

Portraits of a husband & wife, quarter-plate size, by Jeremiah Gurney, a half length portrait of each, he seated facing left w/curly hair & long sideburns, she facing right wearing a bonnet & long-sleeved flowered dress, overall excellent condition, each re-sealed in half cases, New York, New York, ca. 1850s, the pair (ILLUS., bottom of page)............................. **195**

Pair of Portraits of Husband & Wife

Portraits of a husband & wife, quarter-plate size, he shown seated beside a table facing left, wearing checked pants, she also seated beside a table where her bonnet sits, resting her feet on a low stool, glass a little dirty but in cases

w/original seals, England, possibly circa 1840s, the pair (ILLUS.) **600**

Tintypes

Bicyclists Ready to Take Off

Bicyclists, three men in caps seated on bicycles w/men in derby hats standing alongside each as if ready to push them off at start of a race, uncased, 4 x 5" (ILLUS.) **225**

Tintype of a Carpenter & Apprentice

Tintype of Boy Beside a Highwheeler

Boy standing beside his highwheeler bicycle, sixth-plate size, the youth in cycling outfit standing beside his highwheeler, one light bend, overall excellent condition, in full leather case, second half 19th c. (ILLUS.) **160**

Carpenter & his apprentice, quarter-plate size, a studio shot w/the bearded carpenter seated holding some tools & his young apprentice standing to his right, strong tones, very sharp, some emulsion bubbling, in hanging-style half case, late 19th c. (ILLUS.) **85**

Civil War Soldier with Sword

Civil War soldier with sword, carte-de-visite size, young man in Civil War-era uniform & hat stands w/hands crossed in front of him on sword hilt, the back marked "S. Wing's Ferrotype Rooms, only at 290 Washington St., Boston" (ILLUS.) **200**

of Lading" Internal Revenue stamp on reverse, in full case (ILLUS.) **275**

Carte-de-Visite Union Soldier Tintype

Civil War Union infantryman, carte-de-visite size, shown wearing a shell jacket & plug hat, excellent condition, in half case (ILLUS.) **350**
Civil War Union soldier with flag, half-plate size, the young man in uniform standing beside the American flag tinted in red, white & blue, very sharp & well executed, in half of a damaged Union case **1,025**

Tintype of Civil War Union Corporal

Civil War Union corporal, quarter-plate size, a studio pose of a standing gaunt young soldier in uniform, interesting camp scene backdrop, very sharp w/good contrast, mat & preserver but no case (ILLUS.) **302**

Tintype of a Spotted Dog

Dog curled up, sixth-plate size, a large spotted dog curled up on the floor in a studio setting, slightly low contrast, uncased, 19th c. (ILLUS.) **110**

Civil War-era Sailor

Civil War-era sailor, quarter-plate size, man wearing hat at rakish angle & smoking pipe leans on base of pillar in studio setting, the back of tintype w/10-cent "Bill

Tintype Portraits in Thick Union Case

Gentleman & lady, a portrait of a bearded gentleman & a lady, in a triple-thick round brown Union case, case w/very tiny interior chip, mid-19th c. (ILLUS.) **275**

Scarce Early Tennis Themed Tintype

Group of tennis players, by E.L. Merrow, Bethlehem, New Hampshire, a studio pose of a group of young men & woman, four holding tennis racquets, one woman appears to be an African-American, racquets & clothing suggesting the period of 1885-90, great sharpness & contrast, scarce early tennis scene, image 3 1/2 x 5 1/4", mat 4 1/4 x 6 1/2" (ILLUS.) **400**

Group portrait of four young women, sixth-plate size, three seated figures & one standing behind, one woman holding a Holmes-Bates stereo viewer & the others some stereo views, very sharp, near mint condition, ca. 1880s (ILLUS.) **50**

Jockey dressed in his silks, occupational image of the standing jockey beside a small table, very sharp w/great tones, several small scratches on top edge, second half 19th c., image 2 1/2 x 3 3/4" (ILLUS.).. **250**

Four Women with Stereo Viewer & Views

Unusual Jockey Occupational Portrait

Great Tintype of Boy on Rocking Horse

Little boy on his rocking horse, wholeplate size, charming image of a serious young lad seated on his rocking horse, great tones & contrast, flawless condition, in original frame w/very slight wear, from a New York state estate, mid-19th c., oval image 5 1/2 x 7 1/2", frame 12 x 14" (ILLUS.)... **750**

Union Case Holding Tintype of Boy

Little boy with pull toy, ninth-plate size, in oval Union case titled "Serenade," case in excellent condition, mid-19th c. (ILLUS.).. **350**

Little Girl with Toys

Little girl with toys, quarter-plate size, little girl w/long dark hair sitting cross-legged on floor next to child-size chair that holds small doll, other toys strewn on floor around her, in full leather case (ILLUS.) **325**

Unusual Tintype Mounted in Oval Tin

Man standing in studio setting, image of a bearded gentleman standing between a fancy carved chair & an upholstered chair, mounted on the interior lid of what appears to be an oval tobacco tin, the facing lid fitted w/cut-out paper American Express label, image in excellent condition, exterior shows slight signs of use w/fine patina, second half 19th c., exterior 3 3/4 x 5 1/4", 1 1/2" h. (ILLUS.) **200**

Tintype of Man with Kodak Camera

Man with camera, older man standing holding hat in one hat & Kodak No. 3 or No. 3jr. in other, 2 1/2 x 3 1/2" (ILLUS.).............. **450**

Couple with Stereoscope & Views

Man & woman at table, half-plate size, couple sits on either side of a small draped table, the man holding Holmes-Bates stereoscope w/a view, other stereo views on the table between them, uncased (ILLUS.) **150**

Tintype of Chemist or Pharmacist

Occupational - chemist/pharmacist, man standing next to low table that holds bottles & mortar pouring substance from jar into glass container, uncased, 2 1/2 x 3 1/4" (ILLUS.) **163**

Occupational view of an upholsterer, sixth-plate size, a young man in working clothes standing & leaning one arm on the arm of a large sofa, the man holding a claw hammer w/samples of his work around him, strong image slightly dark at the bottom, overall excellent condition, uncased, second half 19th c. (ILLUS.) **80**

Outdoor scene of a man & his high-wheeler bicycle, sixth-plate size, an amusing scene w/one young man standing & leaning on the bicycle while his friend is stretched out on the ground behind him, very sharp w/good tones, excellent condition, second half 19th c. (ILLUS.) **150**

Tintype of Young Man & His Bicycle

Occupational Tintype of Upholsterer

Unusual Outdoor Tintype Scene

Outdoor Tintype of Two Couples in an Open Carriage

Outdoor scene of figure near a house, whole-plate size, a scene w/a pile of wood & a tree in the foreground w/men & women posed on the pile, a small house in the background, framed in an oval mat & a period walnut frame, excellent condition, America, mid-19th c., image 5 1/2 x 7 1/4", frame 9 1/4 x 11" (ILLUS., bottom prev. page) **605**

Outdoor scene of two couples in an open carriage, half-plate size, by H.W. Riffar, Brooklyn, New York, two men in the front seat & two women in the back seat, pulled by a single horse, couple of very minor bends but overall excellent w/sharp focus & good tones, in a worn paper folder marked "H.W. Riffar, 113 and 115 Fourth Street, Brooklyn - Horses and Wagons photographed at shortest notice," second half 19th c. (ILLUS., top of page) **180**

Outdoor view of a large house, half-plate size, a sharp image of a Victorian home w/a nice yard & picket fence located in the Hudson Valley of New York, people can be seen on the front porch, small rust spot on lower edge, otherwise excellent condition, America, second half 19th c. (ILLUS., below) **130**

Nice Exterior View of a Large Victorian House

Post Mortem of a Child Posed on a Cart

Post mortem of a toddler in a wheeled cart, quarter-plate size, the child posed on large pillows resting on a cart w/large wheels, unusual image, excellent condition, in full case (ILLUS.) **225**

Post mortem of an elderly gentleman, sixth-plate size, a half-length view of the man laid in his coffin w/his arms crossed, image a bit dark w/some emulsion crazed

& starting to peel, in half case, mid-19th c. (ILLUS.) **80**

Post Mortem of an Elderly Gentleman

Post mortem portrait, baby wearing long gown lying w/hands folded, unmounted, 2 1/2 x 3 3/4" (ILLUS., below) **150**

Post Mortem Tintype of Baby

Tintype of Men & High-Wheeled Bikes

Two men with high-wheeled bicycles, studio pose of two young men, each standing beside his high-wheeled bicycle, unmounted, excellent condition, late 19th c., image 2 1/4 x 3 1/4" (ILLUS.) **248**

Tintype of Union Soldier

Union soldier, sixth-plate size, man wearing uniform & short cape stands holding Springfield rifle w/fixed bayonet, in full case (ILLUS.) **400**

Union Infantryman with Bayonet

Union infantryman, sixth-plate size, man in Civil War-era uniform & hat holds rifle w/fixed bayonet, in full case (ILLUS.) **300**

Charming Tintype of Young Black Boy

Young African-American boy, ninth-plate size, charming pose of a young boy seated atop a draped stool, excellent condition, mid-19th c. (ILLUS.) **100**

Glossary
of Select Photographic Terms

Types of Photographic Images

Autochrome: A type of positive color transparency patented in France in 1904 by the brothers Auguste and Louis Lumiere. By 1907 it was in commercial use and became the first popular color photo process.

Ambrotype: An early type of photographic image made when a collodian wet-plate negative is mounted in front of a dark surface to produce a positive image. The process was introduced in 1851 and remained popular into the 1860s. It supplanted the more expensive Daguerreotype, but each picture was one of a kind.

Cabinet Card: A photographic print that was mounted on a heavy rectangular card background about 4 1/4 x 6 1/2". The image was produced using a glass plate negative, so multiple copies were possible. Introduced in the mid-1860s, Cabinet Card photos remained popular until about 1900.

Carte-de-Visite: The name means "visiting card" in French, but these were actually very small paper photographs that were mounted on heavy card stock. The term is sometimes abbreviated as "CDV." First introduced in France, these "cartes" became widely popular in the United States by the 1860s. Many notable political and entertainment figures had them produced for distribution to the public, who could include them in albums that also held images of family members and friends. They were replaced by Cabinet Cards by the 1870s.

Daguerreotype: Named for their French inventor, L.J.M. Daguerre, the Daguerreotype was the first practical and widely used method of producing permanent photographic images. The process was invented in 1839 and by the early 1840s had spread to the United States and was widely practiced by professional as well as more amateur photographers. The process produced a one-of-a-kind positive image on a copper sheet that had been specially coated with a light-sensitive silver halide solution which, when exposed to mercury vapor, would produce a detailed image with a silvery reflective surface that had to be protected under glass in special cases. The images were made in a range of sizes, from a double whole plate (8 1/2 x 13") and whole plate (6 1/2 x 8 1/2") down to the sixteenth-plate size (1 5/8 x 2 1/8"). The half-plate (4 1/4 x 6 1/2"), quarter-plate (3 1/4 x 4 1/4"), sixth-plate (2 3/4 x 3 1/4"), and eighth-plate (2 1/8 x 3 1/4") sizes are most commonly found. By the 1860s Ambrotypes and Tintypes had superseded this type of photography.

Tintype (aka Ferrotype): A photographic image produced by using a collodian wet-plate process in which the emulsion was coated on a sheet of black japanned iron (hence "ferro"). When developed, a positive image was produced on the metal sheet. First patented in 1856, the process became widely popular because it was inexpensive. Examples were still being produced into the early 20th century, even after paper photographs were widely available.

Stereo Views: Long rectangular heavy cards mounted with pairs of paper photographic images taken with special stereoscopic cameras. They produced a three-dimensional image when viewed through the stereoscope or stereo viewer. Viewing these images was a popular form of home entertainment from the 1850s into the early 20th century.

Wet Plate photographic process: An early method of producing glass negatives that could allow multiple images of a picture to be made. A sheet of glass was coated with a collodian-based light-sensitive emulsion. When developed, the negative image could be reproduced by using a special albumen-treated paper. The albumen solution was light-sensitized with silver nitrate and applied to a special lightweight paper on which the image was printed. The process was invented in England in 1851.

Later this process was replaced by the **Gelatin Dry Plate** process. In this process a light-sensitive emulsion was again applied to a glass plate but was then allowed to dry before being exposed to light in the camera. It was a simpler process than the wet plate system and was in general use by the 1880s.

Early Viewing Devices

Magic Lantern: An early projection device that generally consisted of a metal box fitted with a small interior fuel-fed lamp that backlit glass slides projected through an adjustable lens at the front. It was very popular for both public and home use from the mid-19th century into the 20th century, when it was replaced by motion pictures.

Graphoscope: A viewing device often combined with a stereoscope. It was an oversized magnifying lens that allowed a very close-up view of cabinet cards and other paper images.

Phenakistascope: A very early "persistence of vision" device that was composed of an upright disk on a handle that was cut with small slits. A special illustrated disk was attached to it; when the disk was spun and viewed through a hand-held mirror, the images gave the appearance of movement.

Praxinoscope: Another early "persistence of vision" device related to the Phenakistascope and Zoetrope. It had a cylindrical drum with small mirrors on a pedestal base. Special animated strips were placed inside the drum; as it was spun, the reflected images on the strip created the illusion of movement.

Zoetrope: Another widely popular "persistence of vision" device that consisted of a deep cylindrical drum cut with thin slots around the sides. Special illustrated animation disks were placed inside the drum; when the drum was spun, the illusion of movement was created.

APPENDIX I
Select List of Camera Manufacturers

The American Camera Company, London, England

Ansco Camera Co., United States

E. & H. Anthony, United States

A. Birnie, Dundee, Scotland

Joshua Billcliff, Manchester, England

Blair Camera Co., United States

Leon Bloch, France

British Ferrotype Company, England

J.T. Chapman, England

Chicago Ferrotype Company, United States

Compagnie Francaise de Photographie, France

Ernemann, Germany

Franke & Heidecke, Germany

Gaumont, Paris, France

Graflex Inc., United States

Walter Griffiths & Co., England

Houghton, England

Huttig, Germany

ICA (Zeiss), Germany

Jeaneret & Cie, Paris, France

F. Jonte, France

Kershaw & Sons, England

Kodak (Eastman Kodak Co.), Rochester, New York

E.B. Koopman, New York, New York

J. Lancaster, England

Le Franceville (L. F. & G.), France

Ernst Leitz (Leica), Germany

J. Lizars, Scotland

London Stereoscopic Company, London, England

Lumiere Bros., France

C. Merville, Paris, France

Minolta, Japan

Monroe Camera Co., Rochester, New York

Newman & Guardia, England

Perken, Son & Rayment, England

Thornton Pickard, England

F. Putnam, New York, New York

Jules Richard, France

Ricoh, Japan

J. Robinson & Sons, England and Ireland

Thomas Ross & Co., England

W. W. Rouch, England

Sanderson Camera Co., England

Scovill Mfg. Company, United States

Seneca Camera Co., Rochester, New York

Stirn Cameras, Germany and New York

Tisdell & Whittelsey, United States

Toyoca Cameras, Japan

Watson & Sons, England

Wollensack & Sons, England

Zeiss, Germany

APPENDIX II
Select List of Stereoscope and Stereo Viewer Makers

R.J. Beck, England

Alexander Beckers, United States

Brewster (refers to style after the original inventor, Sir David Brewster)

J. W. Cadwell, United States

Carpenter & Westley, England

Jules Damoy, France

Jules Dubosc, France

Ernemann, Germany

Gaumont, France

W. J. Gibbons, England

F. J. Ives, United States

Kershaw & Sons, Leeds, England

Keystone View Company, United States

George Knight, England

James Lee, United States

W. H. Lewis, United States

J. Lizars, Glasgow, Scotland

The London Stereoscopic Company, London, England

J. F. Mascher, United States

Francois Mathieu, England

Negretti & Zambra, England

Nelson Chase, United States

Newlands, Calcutta, India

E. K. Page, United States

Hilarious & Lewis Pattberg, United States

A. Quirilo, United States

De Witt S. Rawson, United States

C. J. Rowsell, England

Ebenezer Scott, Scotland

Sealey & Lee, United States

L. D. Sibley, United States

Smith, Beck & Beck, England

Henry Swan, England

Underwood & Underwood, United States

H. C. White, United States

R. R. Whiting, United States